D0108324

10-MINUTE TOUGHNESS

THE MENTAL-TRAINING PROGRAM FOR WINNING BEFORE THE GAME BEGINS

JASON SELK

FOREWORD BY JEFF WILKINS, NFL PRO BOWL KICKER

New York Chicago San Francisco Lisbon London Madrid Mexico City
Milan New Delhi San Juan Seoul Singapore Sydney Toronto

The McGraw·Hill Companies

Library of Congress Cataloging-in-Publication Data

Selk, Jason.
10-minute toughness : the mental-training program for winning before the game begins / Jason Selk
p. cm.
Includes index.
ISBN 978-0-07-160063-7 (alk. paper)
1. Exercise—Psychological aspects. 2. Mind and body. 3. Mental health. I. Title. II. Title : Ten minute toughness.

GV481.2.S57 2009
613.7′1019—dc22 2008009834

1 2 3 4 5 6 7 8 9 10 11 12 13 14 15 16 17 18 19 20 21 FGR/FGR 0 9 8

ISBN 978-0-07-160063-7
MHID 0-07-160063-9

Interior design by Think Design, LLC

This book is printed on acid-free paper.

Contents

Foreword

Jeff Wilkins

When there are two seconds left on the game clock and the difference between winning and losing rests on your ability to kick a football through two uprights that seem to be much farther in the distance than the stats would indicate afterward, it truly takes mental toughness to perform at your best. 10-Minute Toughness is the mental training plan I used to mentally prepare myself for the pressures of playing in the NFL.

I believe that every athlete deserves to learn how to use 10-Minute Toughness. It is easy to understand and actually enjoyable to complete. It helped me focus on exactly what I needed to do mentally to be able to consistently perform under pressure. 10-Minute Toughness helped me keep a high level of confidence and simplify what I needed to stay focused on to kick at my best. It helped me in good times, and it was also a great resource in helping me through tough spots.

When I would line up for a game-winning field goal (or any kick, for that matter), instead of focusing on how important the kick was for my personal and professional goals and my teammates, coaches, and friends (not to mention the collective will of an entire city), I was able to quiet the crowd and opposing team and enter the mindset that allowed me to kick at my best. I was in control of my thoughts, which helped me to have a very successful NFL career.

I contacted Jason Selk about his mental training program because I wanted to learn how my mind could help me play at the highest level possible. I didn't want someone trying to help me with personal issues. Not to say that my life is perfect, but I am a happy, healthy person; have a great family; and have been blessed in many ways. Jason was great in that he really listened to what my goals were and specifically tailored what he did to give me exactly what I wanted.

I can remember on one occasion when the Rams were down by ten points to the Houston Texans with twenty-six seconds left on the game clock. Ryan Fitzpatrick, our third-string quarterback, led the team to a late touchdown to bring us within three points. As I prepared for the onside kick, I remember feeling calm, confident, and focused on exactly what I needed to do. We recovered the kick and the offense miraculously got us in position to tie the game. I would need to make a forty-seven-yard field goal to put us into overtime.

With four seconds left on the Reliant Stadium game clock and my team losing 27–24, I took my steps back, looked up and centered the target, took my steps over and got set, told myself to drive through the ball while my intensity and aggressiveness built, gave the OK to the holder, and the ball was snapped. From forty-seven yards away, I hit it hard and drove the ball right down the middle to send our team into overtime, where we would eventually go on to beat the Houston Texans 33–27 in a thrilling victory.

At the moment right before the ball is snapped—when the stadium is rocking with sixty thousand fans pelting me with every curse and hex they can muster, the opposing coach trying to freeze me, the opposing defense ready to flatten me, and the game on the line—it all comes together: the physical *and* mental training. That's the moment when mental toughness blocks out the noise and focuses my concentration on doing my job to my greatest potential.

The thing that all reporters get wrong when they ask me about "pressure" after the game is, in that one moment, there is no pressure. When I try to explain why, they can't fathom it, but I've been there a thousand times before. In every practice I see myself executing flawlessly, I know the feeling of being calm and aggressive at the same time—where my mind has a pinpoint focus on the one thing I need to do to be successful, where every muscle in my leg fires in sequence as I connect with the ball and send it sailing through the uprights. In my mind I've practiced that kick a thousand times along with another thousand kicks with the game on the line, during the Super Bowl, as the clock expires, or in overtime before the largest audience to ever see a game. Everything after that is a chip shot.

The doubts everyone is curious about, wondering whether they creep into my mind, have no room in my head because I practice controlling my thoughts the same way I practice nailing down my technique. It all becomes routine, and mental toughness is what brings everything together.

10-Minute Toughness is what the title says—ten minutes a day that connect your talents and abilities to the outcome you're seeking. As a retired NFL player looking forward, I can see as many applications in the business world for the toughness Jason Selk's program brought out of me as there were on the football field.

I went to Jason to channel my skills for the big game and give myself the best opportunity to rise to every occasion, but the tools he gave me go beyond extra points and field goals. His teaching—and by extension, this book—puts you at your best when you most need to be there. It shows you how to put your best foot forward each time your number is called. As a kicker, I couldn't ask for much more than that.

Acknowledgments

I would like to personally thank the Ictus Initiative for connecting me to my agent, Farley Chase; Dave Fletcher for his contributions to the writing; Ron Martirano for overseeing the project; and McGraw-Hill for taking a chance on the book. This book is dedicated to all of my coaches: thank you for your knowledge, support, and motivation. Special thanks to Russ and Kathy Telecky, Tracy Steel, and Todd Beyer for teaching me about hard work and commitment. Thanks to Dr. Patrick Stack, Dr. Rocco Cottone, Dr. Kathleen Haywood, and Dr. Marshall Colt for your professional guidance. And a very special thank-you to my parents, Jack and Elizabeth Selk, for being the best coaches a son could ever have.

I also extend a note of gratitude to all the athletes mentioned in this book. I highly value and respect every individual with whom I work, and I honor the tenets of confidentiality that we've established. Athletes cited have afforded me the permission and privilege to tell their stories, which helped transform this manuscript into a living, breathing, functioning tool for individuals aspiring to further success. I am forever indebted to the numerous athletes who allowed me to use their experiences with the 10-Minute Toughness mental-training program in the hopes of helping others achieve their dreams.

Introduction

Uneasiness was creeping onto the faces of the players and coaches in the St. Louis Cardinals' dugout as the bottom of the eighth inning began at Busch Stadium. It was September 30, 2006, just one day before the end of the season, and the upstart Milwaukee Brewers were ahead, 2–0. The Cards were fighting for the National League Central Division crown. Over the past two weeks, they had watched an eight-and-a-half-game lead over the Houston Astros dwindle to just one game. St. Louis needed to win both of its final games to secure the division title and playoff berth.

After notching two outs in the eighth, the visiting Brewers were four outs away from officially spoiling the Cardinals' postseason hopes. The Cardinals had managed to load the bases, when thirty-four-year-old pinch hitter Scott Spiezio stepped into the box. Spiezio, a switch-hitter, knew that the pressure was on and that it was up to him to deliver a key hit in crunch time. Hard-throwing reliever Francisco Cordero quickly got ahead in the count, one ball and two strikes, but Spiezio came up big on the next pitch, stroking Cordero's offering off the top of the right-field wall for a bases-clearing triple that put St. Louis ahead for good, 3–2. The Cardinals would wind up winning the NL Central Division and would go on to win the World Series.

Even though Scott had some off-the-field difficulties after two very productive 2006 and 2007 seasons, he has a great heart and a strong mind. He is capable of a good many things, and I believe the mental toughness he displays on the field will carry over and help him overcome lapses in judgment and make healthy decisions in his personal life as well.

It was a wild finish to the 2006 season for Spiezio, who'd considered retirement after a dissatisfactory 2005 season as a Seattle Mariner. In 2005, Spiezio had just three hits in forty-seven at bats, a .064 batting average for the career .255 hitter. Though he had been the starting third baseman for the world champion Anaheim Angels in 2002, his release from the Mariners after 2005 seemed to imply that his glory days were over. But Spiezio made up his mind to give it another try and see if he could recapture his previous major-league success.

About a week of spring training remained before the start of the 2006 season when Scott contacted me about working with him one-on-one in my 10-Minute Toughness (10-MT) program. At the time, he still didn't know if he would make the team. Scott already had some background with the program from attending a series of three one-hour presentations that I gave to the entire team at the beginning of spring training.

Right from the start, I could tell that Scott was determined to do whatever it was going to take, both physically and mentally, to become a key contributor to the Cardinals. Physically, he had committed to an extensive weight-training regimen that went above and beyond the base program set up by St. Louis's strength coach, Pete Prinzi, and his staff. Mentally, Scott wanted to make sure he was consistently in a frame of mind conducive to meeting all of his goals and getting the results he felt capable of achieving.

For Scott, the result was a season that revived his career. In 276 at bats, he hit .272 (third-highest batting average in his eleven-year career), with thirteen home runs and fifty-two runs batted in. In addition, he was a major contributor to the Cardinals' getting into the 2006 postseason and having great success. It was surprising to some observers but certainly a welcome career resurgence for a veteran who was expected to be a utility player on a team with a deep lineup of talented hitters. In his sixty-one starts, Scott wound up giving the Cardinals the kind of production they would expect from an all-star-caliber player in his prime playing years, and he did it in clutch situations.

Where did this sudden rejuvenation come from? It came from an impressive work ethic that included Scott's identifying his goals and from his diligence in sticking with the process we set up together to help him achieve his definition of success. I did with Scott what I do with all of my clients: quite simply, I asked the questions that needed to be answered in order to make things better for Scott, the baseball player. There were no painstakingly long sessions spent in an office discussing questions like "Can you tell me about your childhood?" The 10-Minute Toughness program is simply about identifying and utilizing a handful of mental tools that are proven to help people perform more consistently.

I choose to relate Scott's story when I talk about my program for two reasons. First, he began seeing the benefits of working with it almost immediately. He had a solid spring training and made the Cardinals' opening-day roster. He completed his mental workouts daily as part of his pregame preparations. For Scott, 10-MT became just as important as taking batting practice or spending time in the weight room. As he put it, "I feel more focused and prepared when I complete my mental work. I think it's every bit as important as the physical work I do, because, more than anything, it helps me keep it simple."

Second, Scott's story highlights the importance of athletes taking care of themselves in their personal lives as well as developing skills and abilities for professional success. It is important to note that mental training, like physical training, can help athletes reach their ultimate goals. However, it is essential for athletes to make good decisions off the field as well. Engaging in healthy relationships and having good nutrition and sleep habits are ever-important pieces of the puzzle. No matter how physically strong or mentally tough a person is, substance abuse is a major obstacle to success.

The Mental Weight Room

Over the last ten years, I've been fortunate enough to work with Olympic gold medalists, NCAA scoring leaders, major-league all-stars, NASCAR drivers, golfers in the PGA and LPGA, NFL Pro Bowlers, and countless other professional and amateur athletes. As a sport psychology consultant, I expect that players will talk with me from time to time about a personal issue other than on-field performance, but I am not some touchy-feely counselor interested in psychoanalyzing athletes' deepest, darkest fears and desires. Nor am I likely to ever spout some Freudian cliché about my clients' id or superego and how the disposition of the personality all relates back to the mother. The truth is that we all have issues in our lives. We don't become adults without developing some baggage along the way. Regardless, I would be making a mistake in assuming that the players with whom I work are interested in my help restoring, rehabilitating, or revitalizing their mental health.

Elite athletes don't want me getting inside their heads and screwing things up. After all, these are people who have cultivated their physical ability to reach the apex of achievement in their sport. In the grand scheme of athletic competition, these players have already enjoyed tremendous success by the time I start talking to them. When presented with the opportunity to work with a sport psychology consultant, they figure there are a whole lot more things that can go wrong than there are things that might go right. What I always try to make clear to the individuals with whom I work, whether athletes or executives, is that my chief aim is to help refine their existing skills more efficiently and consistently than they could do otherwise.

In essence, an athlete who decides to work with me to improve his or her mental game is no different from one who hires a nutritionist to maximize muscle growth. A dietitian or nutrition expert identifies the specific formula of vitamins and protein supplements that will help build an athlete's body to its most efficient form. However, merely hiring a nutritionist won't do much good if that player isn't in the weight room doing the work that will optimize how those carbohydrates and protein shakes affect the body's physical stature and growth.

The same is true for athletes and businesspeople who work with me. My 10-Minute Toughness routine provides competitors of all ages and skill levels with the "nutrients" essential for mind building and strengthening. I am not getting into the heads of the individuals with whom I work—they are getting inside their own heads. I merely steer people in the best direction by asking them the right questions and getting them to think about their goals and identify exactly what it will take to achieve these goals.

I don't pretend to be an expert on any of the sports in which my clients participate, whether it's baseball, football, basketball, gymnastics, or any other activity. Athletes looking for a mental edge don't need another external voice coaching them along. What they do need is to learn how to become their own coach, internally.

A Program Born of Frustration

Concreteness and simplicity are the main points I endeavor to attain in my program. In the years leading up to developing 10-Minute Toughness in 2000, I became frustrated with mainstream sport psychology books. The literature was loaded with excellent concept and theory; however, it lacked a concrete mental-training program to help athletes better control their success. My hands-on experience working with professional and amateur athletes told me that athletes were also frustrated with the lack of a simple, defined mental-training process.

People who wanted to get physically stronger would consult a trainer, and the trainer would provide them with a strength program that included a specific and proven method of getting physically stronger. The strength program would be something like three sets of ten of this exercise, three sets of twelve of that exercise, three sets of eight of another exercise, and so on. A person who follows such a program can't help but get stronger. In contrast, many of the sport psychology books tell you to be mentally stronger but don't provide you with the strength program to fully accomplish the desired mental toughness.

While other sport psychology books do a good job of telling you *what* to think, 10-Minute Toughness will teach you exactly *how* to develop the mental toughness needed to formulate and maintain those productive thoughts. It provides individuals with the details needed to accomplish the development of mental toughness. If you complete the mental-strength program provided here, you cannot help but become mentally tougher.

Athletes want to be told what to do to become better. They seek tangible results that are reflected in their performance. Amazing progress has been made in the field of sport psychology over the last twenty years, yet controlling the mental disposition of athletes today—regardless of skill level—is seemingly as difficult now as ever before. It doesn't have to be. The power lies in the hands (and head) of the athlete. All that's needed are the tools.

The title of this book, *10-Minute Toughness,* implies that in ten minutes, athletes can be mentally prepared for competitive success. Although it seems too good to be true, it's not. An individual who will allot ten minutes per day to focus on mental work will gain the mental edge needed for competitive excellence. Athletes using 10-MT spend approximately four to five minutes after each practice and competition to focus on strengths and goal-related thinking. They also spend five minutes a day completing a five-step mental workout prior to the next day's training and/or competition to help develop a pinpoint focus on what they are trying to improve and what it takes to make it happen.

The 10-MT tools are scientifically proved to enhance the mind's ability to focus on the qualities necessary for improvement and consistency. The real value of 10-MT is that it is simple and concrete enough for athletes and other competitors to understand and to commit to integrating into the daily training routine. Think about it: in just ten minutes a day, you can guarantee that you will be mentally prepared for every practice and competition.

The field of sport psychology has identified self-efficacy (self-confidence) as the most influential mental variable in controlling performance. This means that if you have a strong belief in your ability to perform well, then the chances of your actually performing well greatly improve. This program is specifically designed to help athletes improve self-confidence. The two most effective ways to develop self-confidence are to perform well and to physically and mentally prepare to perform well.

The program works because it has two primary strengths. First, it forces athletes to identify the "process of success." The process of success is a clear and concise assessment of what it takes for the athlete to perform well. This assessment is done daily after training and competition. Second, a mental workout provides a vehicle for mentally training the identified process of success. In addition, athletes visualize success outcomes to enhance self-confidence. They identify the most beneficial thoughts to have and then condition their minds to be able to maintain those thoughts more fully throughout training sessions and competition. It is certainly not rocket science, but it absolutely works!

Essentially, what 10-MT does is provide athletes with a simple and concrete method of focusing the mind and body on precisely what it takes to be successful. Athletes then rehearse the process of success on a daily basis, which strengthens the mind and increases the likelihood of fully realizing their goals.

I have presented the 10-Minute Toughness mental-training plan not only to athletes and coaches but also to business executives and corporate teams, performing artists, and many other types of clients. This book will give you the tools to customize the program for your own needs. Whether you're an aspiring athlete, a middle manager looking to connect better with your team and get ahead, or someone striving for personal fitness, mental toughness is the common source for the drive necessary to bring your goals within reach. I use athletes and competitive sport as my primary examples in the pages that follow, but the principles of mental strength training are the same for competitors on and off the field.

The Three Phases of 10-MT

There are three essential phases in the 10-MT mental-training program. Phase 1 is what I refer to as the mental workout. This individualized mental-training plan helps athletes identify and focus on their "control points," or *what it takes* for success. Athletes learn to consistently maintain mental focus during training and competition by completing the mental workout before stepping onto the field.

As you read through "The Mental Workout" chapters in the first section of the book, you will fill in specific details for each of the tools. These details will likely change over time, so it is important to learn how to use the tools in combination and, as you progress, to feel comfortable changing the details to more specifically tailor the program to your needs. As you will see, the mental workout will become a terrific vehicle for emphasizing and making whatever improvements you desire.

10-Minute Toughness Mental Workout

1. **The Centering Breath.** A fifteen-second deep breath designed to control arousal states.
2. **The Performance Statement.** A specifically tailored self-statement useful for increasing training and competitive focus.
3. **The Personal Highlight Reel.** An advanced form of visualization allowing athletes to increase skill refinement and consistency.
4. **The Identity Statement.** A concrete self-statement proven to enhance self-image and performance confidence.
5. **The Centering Breath.** As in step one, a biologically established relaxation technique used to increase the potential to perform well under pressure.

As you become familiar with the tools, you will have the knowledge and expertise to adjust the mental workout to become more effective. The mental workout takes no more than five minutes to complete and contains five steps, which are covered in depth in Chapters 1 through 5.

Phase 2 comprises developing and utilizing an effective goal-setting program. Typically, when coaches and athletes attempt to create a goals program, it turns out to be an hour of writing down goals at the beginning of the season and then revisiting those goals at the end of the season. The 10-MT goals program teaches athletes and coaches how to enhance motivation and performance by integrating goals into *everyday* training sessions and competition.

Vision clarity: Ultimate goal accomplishment associated with sport.
Product goal: A result-oriented goal that is clearly measurable and is usually most effective if it emphasizes accomplishments in the next twelve months.
Process goal: The daily action needed to accomplish both product- and vision-level goals.
Success Log: Questions that encourage the identification of personal strengths and specific desires for improvement.
Personal Rewards Program Questionnaire: Questionnaire that identifies the athlete's motivational preferences.
Personal incentive style: The motivational preferences of athletes that enhance training and competition intensity.

The 10-MT goals program helps athletes and coaches identify individual and team **vision clarity**, as well as **product goals** and **process goals**. In addition, **Success Logs** are used to improve daily goal emphasis. Athletes also complete the **Personal Rewards Program Questionnaire** to identify the **personal incentive style** that produces the ideal motivational impact for training and competition intensity.

Developing a relentless solution-focused approach is phase 3. I have been fortunate to have worked with some incredibly successful individuals. Whether they are professional athletes or corporate executives, I always try to elicit what those individuals believe to be the top reasons that they have been able to rise above the masses and achieve extraordinary accomplishments. I have noticed that one trait that truly successful people have in common is that they have developed and maintained a solution-focused approach in their careers and in life.

Phase 3 teaches individuals how to develop a relentless focus on solutions. The solution-focused model, **Always have a solution on the board**, is illustrated through real-life narratives and results. Athletes and coaches are able to realize the small difference between good and great by asking, **What is one thing I can do that could make this better?** The solution focus offers a reliable tool for reaching and exceeding one's potential.

Always have a solution on the board: A results-driven model that identifies the biological and environmental obstacles to achieving greatness.

What is one thing I can do that could make this better?: A concrete method of overcoming all obstacles and making success a permanent state.

Thinking Outside the Box

As the St. Louis Cardinals entered the postseason in 2006, a rejuvenated Scott Spiezio was more prepared for success than he had ever been. Physically, he had spent countless hours in the weight room and even more time working on his hitting and fielding. From a mental standpoint, 10-MT had successfully prepared him to manage the postseason pressure.

Spiezio had learned to use centering breaths to control his heart rate and arousal state. His performance statement, "See it; short and compact swing," helped him develop and maintain pinpoint focus on staying calm, recognizing the pitch, and then putting a powerful, short, compact swing on the ball. Spiezio used his personal highlight reel to train himself to believe in his ability to perform well under pressure. He had visualized himself being calm, confident, and successful countless times throughout the season, which helped lead to his triumph in that key eighth-inning at bat against the Brewers. To intensify his work ethic and enhance his self-image, he repeated his identity statement to himself in his daily mental workouts: "I put the work in. I am a dominant major-league hitter."

After defeating the San Diego Padres in the National League Division Series, the Cardinals were down one game to none in the National League Championship Series against the heavily favored New York Mets. In the seventh inning of Game 2, the Mets were ahead by 6–4 and appeared destined to take a commanding two-game lead in the best-of-seven series. With two men on base and two outs, Scott Spiezio once again found himself down to his final strike with the Cardinals' season seemingly hanging in the balance. He had swung and missed on two tough changeups by Guillermo Mota and was expecting another off-speed pitch but instead saw a fastball, which he pulled foul to stay alive.

With Mota keeping him guessing, Spiezio stepped out of the box to regain his composure. "See it; short and compact swing," he told himself as he stepped back into the batter's box. The very next pitch, Spiezio put a short, compact swing on another fastball and crushed it off the right-field wall. He missed a home run by inches, ending up with a triple that drove in two runs to tie the game. The stunned New York Mets were unable to recover, and Spiezio doubled in another run in the ninth inning.

The Cardinals went on to beat the Mets in a physically grueling yet unquestionably memorable seven-game series. Eventually, St. Louis would ride the momentum to a World Series championship over the Detroit Tigers. The so-called experts hadn't given the Cardinals much of a prayer against the Tigers, who were coming off a dominating series sweep to capture the American League pennant. Of course, there weren't too many people giving Spiezio a chance of such a career revival, either. For Spiezio and the 2006 Cardinals, numbers could not relate the entire story. The team did not listen to what other people thought, because that was not important. What is important for athletes is to focus on the process of success and what it will take to reach their goals. The 10-Minute Toughness workout gives athletes the focus that they need to reach their potential and beyond.

PHASE 1

THE MENTAL WORKOUT

CHAPTER 1

Centering Breaths

Controlling Your Biology

There are five steps in the 10-Minute Toughness mental workout. The steps take varying times to complete depending on the athlete, but each is vital in its own way. Some sport psychologists recommend performing this workout either before going to bed or after waking up in the morning, and that's how some athletes do it. I know of athletes who believe that by performing the steps before bed, they can influence the dream state and thereby become more effective. However, my clients and I have found that the best results are achieved when the workout takes place within sixty minutes prior to every practice or competition.

Solid Foundation of Mental Strength

When I first developed this program, I emphasized game day more than training days. My original goals were to get athletes to use centering breaths, positive self-talk, and visualization in competition. For example, I worked with a promising high school wrestler who had all the requisite raw skills but who suffered from competition anxiety. Before matches, he would get himself so worked up that he would begin to sweat profusely, he would get dizzy, his stomach would hurt, and at times he would even hyperventilate. His head was spinning so fast before competition that he had no chance once the match began.

In our first session, I taught him how to use centering breaths and various relaxation techniques to help him control the anxiety he experienced before competition. For two months, we worked on mental skills designed to relax him in competition, but things were not improving for this talented wrestler. With my eye on competition day, I told him to take more centering breaths and to focus more on using his relaxation tools just prior to the start of the match.

Finally I decided to emphasize developing a firm basis of mental strength, more like what a weight-training program does for the body. I came up with a mental-training program that would give this young man a foundation of mental strength so that on competition day, rather than his mind being an obstacle to him, it would be an asset. What he needed was to *develop* mental toughness in training, as opposed to trying to use mental tools as a Band-Aid during competition.

An analogy illustrates my point. Imagine that you are a baseball player, and it's the bottom of the ninth inning of Game 7 of the World Series. Visualize yourself as the starting left fielder for your favorite team. You are up to bat with your team behind by one run, with two outs. With teammates at second and third, all you need is to get a base hit, and you and your team will be world champions.

Before the season began, you hired the best track coach in the country to teach you the most effective running techniques. All season, you have been working on your running form, and as you stand in the batter's box, you have all the techniques of running form mastered. There is just one problem: you have not done any strength training for your legs. Although you have the technical tools of running figured out, you have minimal leg strength.

As you face the opposing team's dominant closer, you direct all your energy to getting a hit. On the first pitch, you get your pitch and put a solid swing on it, but you are just a little out in front, and the ball is hit sharply to the third baseman. You realize it is going to be a close play at first, and you hustle out of the batter's box. You focus on your running form and try with all your might to beat the throw, but the leg strength is just not there, and you are thrown out at first.

Now let's take a different training approach for the same situation. It's still the bottom of the ninth of Game 7 of the World Series, with the same score and runners on base. Again, all you need is a base hit to make you and your team world champions.

The difference is that before the season began, you hired a strength coach to help you develop your leg strength and speed, which complemented the work you've done with your track coach. Every day of the season, you have worked diligently at developing the leg strength needed for speed, and as you stand in the batter's box, you are stronger and faster than you have ever been.

As you face the opposing team's dominant closer, you put all your energy into getting a hit. On the first pitch, you see your pitch and put a solid swing on it, but you are just a little out in front, and the ball is hit sharply to the third baseman. You realize it is going to be a close play at first, and as you hustle out of the batter's box, you don't need to think about running fast, because the strength and speed are already there for you. Before you know it, you feel yourself touching first base, and you hear the wild reaction of the crowd. Fans are chanting your name as your teammates cross home plate, and your team wins the game.

While the analogy is a bit dramatic, it is this concept that led me to create a mental-training program fashioned like a concrete, itemized weight-training program. I have found that the athletes who do the 10-MT mental workout every day before practices and games are the ones who then have the mental strength needed for mental control in competition. Even the business executives who follow my mental workout proceed to acquire the tools to better hold their own in the corporate jungle. Once the mental strength is developed, individuals can readily decide what tools to call on for different situations. I no longer concern myself as much with what tools athletes use on game day. I know that if athletes will commit to completing the mental workout as part of their practice routine (a minimum of four days per week during the season), they will effectively begin using their mental tools and strength during competition.

Eventually the wrestler and I figured out that it was best for him to complete the mental workout before practices and strive to develop the mental ability needed to better deal with competition. A couple of years later, the wrestler received a Division I college scholarship for wrestling. He sent me an e-mail after his freshman year and told me he was still doing his mental workout every day before practice. He said his teammates used to laugh and say that when he was doing his mental workout, he was going to his "happy place." After his sterling freshman year, though, those same teammates who were once laughing at him asked him to teach them how to do the mental workout so they could get to their happy place.

Pressure Is More than Butterflies

Athletes at all levels experience pressure during competition. Feeling nervous is a biological inevitability, whether a player is standing on a free-throw line, a pitching rubber, or the fairway of a golf course. This anticipation—or what is often referred to as "a case of the butterflies"—is natural and can fill a player with vivacity and adrenaline, but pre-competition nerves become a hindrance when an athlete does not know how to adequately control the body's ability to prepare for success.

From a scientific standpoint, one of the first things that occurs when a person feels pressure is the acceleration of the heart rate. The increased heart rate frequently causes people to rush what they are doing. This is why people tend to talk faster when they are nervous. On the athletic field, the same thing happens. A player who gets nervous will speed things up, and this typically will have a negative impact on performance. An effective way to control heart rate is to use a "centering breath" before and during competition. The centering breath, often referred to as a "diaphragm breath," is a long, deep inhalation of air into the diaphragm. Inhaling air into the diaphragm is a biological tool that helps control the heart rate. Taking a deep, centering breath allows individuals to keep their heart rate under control and perform at a more effective pace. Easy enough, right? Well, unfortunately it's not so easy.

About five years ago, I had taught one of the major-league pitchers with whom I was working to take a centering breath any time two opposing players got on base. In his next outing, he began the game with two scoreless innings. Then, he caught a bad break in the third inning when a bloop hit fell in for a single in shallow left field. He became noticeably irritated and walked the next batter. With no one out and two men on base, the television camera zoomed in on him. It was obvious to viewers that the young pitcher was angry with himself. He was shaking his head and talking to himself under his breath.

As I watched the situation unfolding, I found myself talking to the television screen. "Step off the mound and take a centering breath," I said, hoping the pitcher would somehow telepathically respond to my pleas. The next batter came up and hit a long fly ball off a pitch that hung up in the strike zone. The left fielder caught the ball at the warning track for the first out. Again, the camera closed in on the pitcher; this time, there was a look of relief on his face as he took a deep breath that lasted three seconds. Now my plea became louder, and I stood up to yell at the TV, "Step off the mound and take a longer, centering breath!" Four of the next five hitters reached base, and the pitcher was eventually pulled from the game after giving up five runs in four innings.

Afterward, when he and I spoke, I asked him why he had not used the deep, centering breath we had talked about. His answer was, "I thought I did." A centering breath is not the same as a normal deep breath. The centering breath should be a deep, cleansing breath that slows the heart rate. A three-second breath does not fit the bill, because air must enter the diaphragm for a true centering breath to work its magic.

Centering Breath = Diaphragm Breathing

I have tried to simplify diaphragm breathing by qualifying a good centering breath as one that lasts fifteen seconds. The formula is 6-2-7: breathe in for six seconds, hold for two, and breathe out for seven seconds. Individuals under the age of twelve should try to have the centering breath last eleven seconds (4-2-5). I have found that if players take a deep breath that lasts fifteen seconds, they will in fact get air into the diaphragm, and the heart rate will slow. My personal findings indicate that attaching time to the centering breath is more effective than monitoring oneself getting air into the diaphragm. It is much easier to count to fifteen than it is to determine whether air has entered the diaphragm.

Make sure as you're taking centering breaths to count a full fifteen seconds. Remember that when you are in a pressure situation, you will feel like rushing the breath. This is when you truly need it the most. If you can't maintain the full fifteen seconds, that is a sure indication that you need to take another one. Stay at it until you can get the fifteen-second centering breath. If you need to, imagine a stopwatch ticking off the full fifteen seconds.

> **Arousal state:** The level of energy or excitement an athlete experiences during performance.

One core aspect of training is known as arousal control. The heart rate is a primary control of a person's **arousal state**. It is important to control heart rate because using the mind effectively becomes increasingly more difficult as the heart rate rises. Once the rate gets to 120 beats per minute, the mind will not be nearly as sharp (unless proper conditioning and mental training has occurred), and at about 150 beats per minute, the mind will essentially shut down and go into survival mode. (In this state, even the best athletes will lose the ability to maintain mental acuity.) Additionally, an elevated heart rate increases arousal states. Athletes need to learn to control heart rate and arousal so that energy supplies are more present in the action moments of training and performance.

Playing with Heart

A punter with whom I worked in the NFL used to have trouble catching the snap before delivering his kick. He would get nervous just before the play and would bobble the football at times, which hurt the quality of his punts. The speed of an oncoming rush of extremely large professional football players will do that to a kicker. Not only is a punter staring at eight or nine players rushing at him full speed, but also he must think about doing his job flawlessly—all in the span of about three seconds.

This particular player found that if he visualized taking a good centering breath right before the ball was snapped in his mental workout, then he was much more likely to take that same good centering breath in reality just before the ball was snapped. This discovery allowed him to be much more at ease and to slow the procedure down to the desired pace. His hand-to-foot times (the amount of time that elapses from when the punter catches the ball to when his foot contacts the ball) sped up, and his hang times (the amount of time the ball is in the air after the punter kicks it) increased as a result of his using the centering breath in his mental workout as well as just before kicking.

The best performances generally occur when the arousal state and heart rate are the same or similar in training and in competition. Many times, the heart rate in training is far lower than it is in competition. This change in arousal between competition and training usually has adverse effects on performance. With this in mind, it is a priority for athletes to learn to control heart rate so that training and competition arousal states are similar.

A client who is a collegiate golfer had this to say: "It's weird, because hitting balls on the range is easy for me; ninety percent of the time, my swing feels great, and the ball goes right where I want it to. When I get out on the course, I start thinking about results, and the next thing I know, I'm uptight, and I can't find my swing. That's when I use my centering breaths. It's still not as easy as it is on the range, but it definitely helps me relax and find my swing."

At rest, an athlete's heart rate is typically between 60 and 70 beats per minute. In anaerobic sports such as golf, gymnastics, and diving, athletes may experience a heart rate of 90 to 100 beats per minute when training. When the same athletes in anaerobic sports are feeling competitive pressure, the heart rate may be as high as 120 to 140 beats per minute. The increased heart rate makes it more difficult to repeat training success. This is one of the main reasons that athletes experience inconsistency in competition.

In the early 1990s, a study was performed on the men's golf team at a Division I university. The golfers were first hooked up to electrodes and heart monitors, and baseline putting-success percentages were established. Each golfer was then asked to try to match or beat his previously determined baseline. If the golfer could accomplish this feat, he would receive a small amount of money. What became obvious was that the heart rates of the golfers were going up and the success rates were going down.

Next, the researchers increased the amount of money in the kitty. As the money increased, the heart rates also increased, and the performances got worse. Then the researches invited the crew of a popular television show to come in, with all the lights and cameras, and record the goings-on for the whole world to view. Again, the heart rates of these elite-level golfers rose, and the performances continued to plummet.

The results of the study affirmed what the researchers already suspected to be true: only a small amount of pressure (in this case, money) is required to dramatically affect heart rate or arousal. If the heart rate in competition is significantly different from the training rate, performance ability typically suffers. What we need to learn to do is prepare for competition in training by increasing arousal states of normal, day-to-day practices and to deal with competition by controlling this pressure or arousal state in the competition setting. The centering breath is a biological tool to help accomplish this task.

Mike Mussina, a major-league pitcher with more than 250 victories in the regular season and postseason combined, discussed the importance of controlling arousal states in Bob Rotella's book *The Golfer's Mind: Play to Play Great.*[1] He said that when he was a kid, his dad put a strike zone on their barn and built him a mound sixty feet away. When he would pitch to the strike zone on the barn, he would imagine he was pitching in the major leagues. He would project himself pitching well in various pressure situations.

When Mussina went from Baltimore to play for the Yankees, the local press asked him how he was going to handle the pressure of pitching under the scrutiny of the

New York stage. He calmly and confidently answered that when he was a kid, he often imagined himself pitching well in the most important games. Now as an adult pitching in those games, he imagines himself hurling to the strike zone on the barn. Mike has thus come up with a way to increase the pressure and arousal in practice and decrease it in games. Perhaps Mike Mussina doesn't need centering breaths as much because he planted the seeds for confronting that kind of pressure at an early age. Many of us don't have the mental toughness of Mike Mussina, so it seems to be highly effective to prepare yourself to deal with pressure prior to competing and to have a functional method of controlling arousal during competition. The centering breath will be a great tool to help you deal effectively with pressure.

CHAPTER 2

The Performance Statement

Simple and Concrete

Early in the year 2000, Sean Townsend had established himself as one of the United States' best male gymnasts, and he was poised to show the world that he was a major force to be reckoned with. In 2001, he collected his first gold medal at the World Championships and placed in the top ten twice in World Cup competitions, identifying himself as a serious medal contender for the 2004 Olympic Games.

Just as Sean was beginning to prepare for his Olympic run, a knee injury derailed his training. He was disheartened at having worked so hard for so long only to have his dreams dashed so quickly. Inadequate training brought on by nagging injuries dropped Sean out of the international spotlight. It appeared as though Sean Townsend's gymnastics career might be over. Then in June of 2006, with the support of his coach, Kevin Mazieka (also the Olympic team coach), he decided to recommit to his training and make another run at his Olympic dream.

In November 2006, I traveled to Houston to help Sean and Kevin implement the 10-Minute Toughness training program as a complement to the intense physical preparation Sean was undertaking. Watching Sean and Kevin train is unforgettable. They both approach their work with unheralded passion. Although neither is shy about getting to the point, they seem to have an unspoken language through which they can express deep concern and pride. As I watched them work together in practice, I noticed true commitment and perseverance.

Coach Mazieka was able to strike a balance between pushing and supporting. At one point, he jumped all over Sean for not paying enough attention to detail while working on what seemed like impossible moves on the pommel horse. The coach pleaded with the twenty-eight-year-old to keep his elbow straighter at the critical moment of the skill. Kevin's attention prompted Sean to push harder on the next turn. Just minutes later, Kevin was there to praise Sean's effort even though the gymnast had just fallen on his dismount. It was clear to me that the coach and athlete respect each other wholeheartedly. Coach Mazieka talks about Sean with the pride a father has for a son: "Sean is a very special talent. He works very hard, and he is a terrific young man."

On February 8, 2007, Sean Townsend and his trusted coach walked into the Las Vegas Sports Complex for the first of two national competitions to select the Senior National Team, which represents the Untied States in all world and Olympic competitions. This time around, things were different: Townsend was not the odds-on favorite. In fact, few insiders believed he had the ability to climb back to the top of the podium. Townsend surprised the field on the first day of competition by fighting his way to a third-place finish.

With Sean almost two points out of first place, he and Kevin discussed strategy for the final day's competition. Many people thought Townsend would play it safe in the finals and feel satisfied with finishing anywhere in the top six. (Similar to a golfer laying up instead of going for the green on an approach shot, gymnasts sometimes eliminate particularly difficult skills from a routine if they have built a lead that they do not want to risk relinquishing.) Townsend and Mazieka had a different plan. With Sean's revitalized training and confidence, they both knew he was good enough to win the competition, and that is exactly what they set out to accomplish.

On the second day of competition, after making up ground on the first four events, Sean was in striking distance with two events remaining. All he needed to do was stay with what had brought him to this point. He had the momentum, and the other athletes were now watching in amazement as he competed with supreme confidence. Sean had discovered that part of his problem over the last three years was that he had been focusing more and more on results rather than on staying in the moment and executing one skill at a time, one routine at a time.

As part of his 10-MT mental workout, Sean created a performance statement to help him stay in the moment. A performance statement is a specifically designed form of self-talk. Self-talk is the conversation that goes on in a person's head throughout the day. It is said that the average person has up to sixty thousand thoughts per day—that's a lot of self-talk. The unfortunate thing about those thoughts is that the majority tend to embody self-doubt or negativity. If we do not choose our thoughts carefully, they can (and many times do) have a negative impact on performance.

Going into the final two events, Sean realized that he was starting to get ahead of himself in thinking about results. He forced himself to concentrate on his performance statement: "One skill at a time, one routine at a time." High bar was Sean's next event. It was both his strongest and most difficult event. For the previous three months, Sean had been using his mental workout to train his mind to stay focused on "one skill at a time," and the effect was obvious as he moved through his high-bar routine almost flawlessly. With one event to go, Townsend was virtually tied for first place with one of the country's most talented and determined young gymnasts. It was the classic showdown of the old veteran taking on the young phenom. Townsend maintained his thought process, and after completing an inspiring floor exercise, he eventually went on to win the competition and claim the top spot on the Senior National Team.

Thinking Through Performance

From a mental standpoint, the most tried-and-true way to increase performance is to improve confidence. Self-talk is one of the most influential agents for honing self-confidence. Extensive research in the sport psychology world confirms that an athlete's internal dialogue significantly influences performance. Athletes who have negative self-talk will generally experience poor performance; conversely, when athletes keep their minds focused on positive performance cues, they are more likely to experience success.

In 1985, tennis great Ivan Lendl had a record of nine wins and twelve losses against John McEnroe. To improve his chances for success against McEnroe, Lendl decided to improve his self-talk. He began repeating to himself daily, "I look forward to playing John McEnroe," and over the next six years, Lendl beat McEnroe ten times while only losing three times.[1]

Pete Sampras, another tennis superstar, said that positive self-talk was a definite help to him in working through adversity and tough points. Sampras would tell himself to "stay focused on the present" and "prepare for the next point" rather than letting his thoughts swirl and become negative.[2]

The benefits aren't limited to the gym and tennis court. In preparation for the Ironman World Championships, one athlete had this to say after achieving her best time and finishing fourth in the world: "Training the positive self-talk for a few months allowed me to focus only on myself and what was going on in my body and mind in sync. . . . The tangible rewards were a huge perk for me, but the real treasures of that race were my newfound ability to use my self-talk tools and remain in the moment."[3]

A performance statement is a type of self-talk designed to help athletes zoom in on one specific thought to enhance performance consistency. It is a simple, yet concrete, thought that specifically identifies the process of success, or what it takes to perform at your best. As you read through the next pages, think about the one core thought that puts you in the best position to play at your peak when you focus on it. For some sports it will make sense to have more than one performance statement.

For the baseball player, there may be a performance statement to emphasize hitting (track the ball, smooth and easy) and defense (set, stay down, watch it into the glove). A basketball player may choose to combine both offense and defense into one performance statement (hustle every possession; attack every rebound; drive, drive, drive), while the gymnast may have a performance statement for every event she competes on (floor: quick hands, tight legs, squeeze; vault: top speed, feet in front; bars: hollow handstands and elbows locked).

The key is to identify the single most fundamental idea of what it takes for you to be successful to allow you to simplify the game. Keeping it simple will allow you to free your mind and body from complications and distractions and play loose with great confidence and passion. As we reach the end of the chapter, I will ask you some very specific questions to help you identify the exact performance statement best suited for you.

"Don't" thinking: An ineffective series of thoughts in which the athlete focuses on what he or she does not want to do rather than on what should be done.

It is highly beneficial for athletes to know what to think as they are preparing for competition. Many times during training and competition, an athlete will experience what I call **"don't" thinking**. In "don't" thinking, people tell themselves what not to do. For example, a hockey player with whom I work used to tell himself, "Don't screw this up, don't swing too hard, and don't hit the ice before the puck." This type of thinking is not helpful, because by directing the mind to what is not supposed to be done, it increases the likelihood that the athlete will feel stress and anxiety. This state, in turn, makes it harder to pay attention to the task at hand, and thus people are more prone to do exactly what they were hoping to prevent.

Mental clutter is another impediment to clear thoughts among athletes. Mental clutter is all the stuff that goes through the mind that interferes with important thoughts about the performance. For the majority of athletes, mental clutter usually occurs because individuals do not know what they should be thinking. Even athletes who have been instructed on what to think have trouble at times because they haven't trained their minds to maintain a specific focus under pressure. Performance statements help athletes stay focused and perform at their best when it counts the most.

Now as the aforementioned hockey player prepares for training and competition, he says to himself, "Relaxed and smooth; my shot is compact and powerful." When he stays relaxed, it helps him to play his game and stay within himself. He knows that if he keeps his mind on "relaxed and smooth," he is better able to avoid all "don't" thinking and mental clutter. In his first year of using 10-Minute Toughness, his scoring percentage increased from 8 percent to almost 30 percent.

Leading with Your Mind

Mental toughness is abnormal, just as physical strength is abnormal. We are born without much muscle development. As we grow, if we don't emphasize physical fitness, we will not develop appreciable strength. In that sense, it is somewhat abnormal to be physically strong. The same is true for mental toughness: most people don't commit to replacing their negative thoughts with positive thinking.

In my opinion, the essence of mental toughness is the ability to replace negative thinking with thoughts that are centered on performance cues or that contribute to improved self-confidence. The more often negative thoughts are replaced with positive self-talk, the more successful and mentally tough a person will be. An athlete's body listens to what the mind tells it. If the mind has up to sixty thousand thoughts a day, and normal thinking is filled with self-doubt and/or negativity, imagine the impact on performance.

It is important for athletes to identify the thoughts that produce consistently strong performance. Once players figure out what those thoughts are, they can train their minds to focus only on those thoughts during competition. George Brett, the Hall of Fame baseball player, used to tell himself, "Try easier," as a reminder to use a smooth and easy swing at the plate. Although this process sounds simple enough, it can be difficult to pull off, especially while under competitive pressure. The mental workout is a structured and concrete method of identifying and controlling the positive self-talk necessary for peak performance.

While it is not a revelation to most people that they should avoid negative thinking, how many of us truly know what we are supposed to think about? The most helpful method to stop self-doubt and negative thinking is thought replacement. Effective thought replacement occurs when you decide what you want to have happen and then think more often about what it will take to make it happen. Whenever unproductive thoughts ("don't" thinking or mental clutter) infringe, replace them with productive ones.

Replace all thoughts of self-doubt or negativity with thoughts of what it is that you want, and you will be much more likely to have those things occur. If you do this as often as possible, your life will be more enjoyable, and you will markedly improve your odds of reaching or exceeding your potential. It is helpful to construct some specific positive self-talk statements prior to facing adversity so that your mind is more practiced and able to use positive thinking when it is most needed.

Thought Replacement

During spring training, I started working with a minor-league pitcher in the St. Louis Cardinals organization who used to believe he had trouble getting left-handed hitters out. Whenever a lefty would come up to the plate, he would think, "I always have trouble against lefties." He would then tense up and have more difficulty finding the strike zone. This made it easier for left-handed hitters to enjoy success against him. Soon scouting reports started reflecting the pitcher's problem with left-handed hitters. Opposing managers were stacking their lineups with lefties, and the left-handed hitters were growing in confidence when they would face this once feared pitcher.

The pitcher became aware of his destructive thought pattern and the necessity to change it. He began replacing his original thought, "I always have trouble against lefties," with his performance statement: "Stay back; pitch for contact." He was telling himself to keep his weight back, which helped him keep the ball down in the strike zone. Pitching for contact enabled him to be more aggressive. Instead of trying to throw the perfect pitch, he now concentrated on throwing a quality, well-located pitch in the strike zone.

Gradually, the pitcher gained more and more success against lefties, and it all started with replacing his unhelpful self-talk with a practical performance statement. Anytime the pitcher realized that he was thinking about how hard it was to pitch to left-handed hitters, he would replace that musing with "Stay back; pitch for contact." This technique allowed him to hone in on the one action that helped him to pitch at his best. By the end of the season, the pitcher had lowered his earned run average (a measure of how may runs a pitcher allows per nine innings) against lefties by a full run and was invited to major-league spring training the next year. He commented, "By the way I am pitching, I know I can dominate at the major-league level. It's just a matter of time."

The key to using thought replacement in sports is to identify what thought is most helpful for performance. If you determine what you want to accomplish in any given situation and then lock your mind on what it takes to achieve that goal, you will have a much better chance of reaping the rewards. This is true in any setting—business, sport, or even social. As often as possible, choose to think about the path to success rather than the obstacles in your way. You have to decide what you want and then put your energy into acquiring it. Don't wait for good luck to find you. Go out and create your own luck.

The only reliable method of overcoming self-doubt and negative thinking is to supply something else for your mind to process. That is where the performance statement comes in. The performance statement serves two principal purposes. First, it is a way to avoid self-doubt, negativity, or mental clutter. Second, it helps you perform at your best by directing your thoughts toward targeted areas of strength. Performance statements enable you to stop dwelling on elements that make it harder for you to perform and start thinking about what helps.

Dominant Self-Talk

Recognizing that you must eliminate self-doubt or negativity is only half the battle. Unfortunately, following through can be a tricky undertaking. Try this quick exercise: Don't think about a pink elephant with blue running shoes. Don't let a pink elephant with blue running shoes cross your mind. Do not picture a pink elephant with blue running shoes. . . . What happened? Did you think about a pink elephant with blue running shoes? Of course you did. The only way you wouldn't have thought about a pink elephant with blue running shoes would have been by focusing completely on something else.

Cognitive psychology has taught us that the mind can fully focus on only one item at a time. For instance, if you were intently focused on a red and white hot-air balloon, you could have avoided thinking about the pink elephant. In short, if you are thinking about what is going wrong in your life, you cannot be thinking about what it takes to make it right. The most effective way to avoid self-doubt and mental clutter is to replace the negative thoughts with specific positive thoughts. The performance statement is an individually tailored positive self-talk statement. It will keep your mind trained on success and what it takes to get there.

I will give you two more examples of performance statements and how they help. I worked with a major-league player who wanted to improve his ability to hit the outside pitch. He developed the following performance statement for hitting: "Relax; look away; go away." He was telling himself to stay loose (it is important for him to swing nice and easy even though he is a power hitter), look for the ball on the outside part of the plate, and then hit to the opposite field. This player had little trouble hitting the inside pitch, so he thought that if he could train himself to hit better to the opposite field, he would have much greater overall success. He was right; his ability to hit to the opposite field improved, and his batting average rose twenty points in one season.

A cyclist client has the performance statement "Weight back and breathe easy." He is teaching himself to concentrate on keeping his weight back so that he can more aggressively use his legs to turn the wheels. Also, he knew he had a tendency to get overexcited, which sped up his breathing and, over the course of the ride, cost him large amounts of energy.

Make sure your performance statement keeps you in a positive mind-set. An obvious way to do this is to avoid using the word *don't*. For example, the cyclist who often gets too pumped up before a race does not tell himself, "Don't get overexcited" or "Don't put your weight forward." Instead, he maintains the proper frame of mind by reminding himself what he needs to do.

Your Performance Statement

As I said earlier, it is advantageous to create your performance statement before facing problems in training or competitions. You can better identify the best way to think when you aren't already in a negative emotional state. To create your personalized performance statement, you need to single out your specific process of success.

Up to this point, the discussion has featured mostly athletes and thus has been weighted toward technical execution. If you instead are using 10-MT to further develop your business career, you might shape your statement around effective communication or negotiation techniques. Here is an example of a performance statement for an executive with whom I work: "Listen first; then decide; be swift and confident." She uses her performance statement to remind herself to listen to her team and clients before making decisions and then to move steadily ahead.

Similarly, if you are using this program to help you maintain a personal fitness routine and get in shape, then your performance statement might highlight your commitment and dedication or the routine itself. A client trying to prioritize exercise had this as his performance statement: "Three days on, one day off; dedicated and committed; I clear my own path." His highlights aren't as much about the technical aspects of doing it right as they are about his desire and ability to be healthy.

Always use what *you* think works when creating your performance statement. The best method I know of to identify your process of success is to answer the following questions (you can use the space provided throughout to record your answers):

1. Imagine that you are about to compete in the biggest game of your life, and the best coach you have ever had is standing right next to you. Sixty seconds before the competition begins, your coach looks you in the eye and tells you that if you stay focused on this one thing or these two things, you will be successful today. What one or two things would the coach name? (Be as specific as possible, and remember to avoid using the word *don't*.)

   ____

   ____

2. Again, imagine that you are about to compete in the biggest competition of your life, but this time, you are both the coach and the athlete. Sixty seconds before the competition begins, you, the coach, look at you, the athlete, and relate that if you stay focused on this one thing or these two things, you will be successful today. What one or two things would you, the coach name? Your response to this question may very well be the same as your answer to the previous question; however, if there is a difference, trust yourself. Remember that

you are truly the expert on what you need to do to be successful.

You need to decide how many performance statements you would like to develop. Most athletes pick the one most important aspect for them to focus on, creating and using only one performance statement. Some choose to use two or more performance statements: gymnasts and divers typically elect to create one performance statement for each event or dive; basketball and baseball players may want to create them for offense and defense; golfers may create one performance statement for putting and another for all other swings; tennis players might have one specific to the serve and one for ground strokes.

A conversation I had with a player on the St. Louis Cardinals while developing his performance statement may help you with this concept. He felt his current hitting coach was the best coach he had ever worked with, so I asked him to imagine that he was about to play in Game 7 of the World Series, and, sixty seconds before the game began, his coach looked him in the eye and said that if he would focus on one thing that day—just this one thing—on every single pitch, he would be successful. I asked him what that one thing was. Although it was difficult for him to imagine at first, he said the coach would tell him to trust himself, look for his pitch, and then attack.

Then I asked him to imagine that he was in the same situation, Game 7 of the World Series, and had been cloned to be not only the athlete but also the hitting coach. Sixty seconds before the game began, his hitting coach self looked at his player self and said, "If you focus on this one thing before every pitch, you and I both know you will be successful." I asked him what he would say to himself in that situation.

Although this was even tougher for him to imagine, he thought that he would tell himself to see the ball and hit it. When I asked him what it took for him to see the ball, he replied, "Seeing the ball is so important for me. I mean really see the ball and then just focus on swinging short and easy. When I think short and easy on my swing, it actually produces a more powerful swing than when I try to overpower things. The key for me is to concentrate on picking the ball up early and then just swinging short and easy."

He thought that picking the ball up early was more helpful than seeing the ball and that finding his swing—short and easy—put him in the best position to hit the ball. "Loading" early was also an essential part of this process, so he initially thought his performance statement would be "Load early, pick it up, short and easy." So I asked him to put himself back in Game 7 of the World Series, seeing himself on deck and digging into the box with the whole world watching. But this time he was to imagine that his mind was focused on only one thing: Load early, pick it up, short and easy.

He imagined the at bat but decided he didn't like the part about loading early and instead went with "Pick it up early, short and easy." In doing so he felt good: "I was relaxed and confident and felt exactly how I would want to." After I asked him how the at bat went he replied, "I hit a game-winning double off the wall; it was awesome!"

Now take a moment and create your own performance statement. Think back to the previously mentioned scenario where you are about to compete in the biggest competition of your life. What do you think would be the one most productive thing for you to be focused on? Remember to have your performance statement(s) reflect what it takes to perform well. Once you decide how many performance statements you are going to use, go ahead and write them down. I have included a few lines to write in, in case you want to have more than one performance statement. Remember, keep it simple and identify the one core thought that allows you to play at your best.

Performance statement: ______________________________

Performance statement: ______________________________

Performance statement: ______________________________

Performance statement: ______________________________

Performance statement: ______________________________

Performance statement: ______________________________

For all athletes, knowing what to think always beats letting thoughts naturally occur. Remember that letting your mind have its way can often cripple you with self-doubt or negativity. Your body listens to what your mind tells it. If you are thinking about all the things that could go wrong, you are making it more likely that things *will* go wrong. On the other hand, if you replace all self-doubt and negativity with your performance statement (or some other form of positive self-talk), you are more likely to achieve the goal of playing at or beyond your potential.

Emphasizing your performance statement by including it in your mental workout will condition your mind as to how to think. The more often that athletes complete their mental workout including their performance statement, the more faithfully they remember to focus on what it takes to be successful in training and competition. Sean Townsend feels that his performance statement is invaluable to his newfound success as one of the United States' top male gymnasts. "My mental training has given me the confidence I need to really go after my dreams as a gymnast," he remarked. "If I take it one skill at a time, I like my chances."

With the accomplishment of making the Senior National Team, Sean and Kevin set their sights on the 2008 Olympics in Beijing. Just a few years earlier, Sean's knee injury called into question what his future held as a competitive gymnast, but Sean kept things simple with his performance statement, "One skill at a time, one routine at a time."

Athletes should try to emulate Sean's approach as much as possible, because it prevents "don't" thinking from affecting performance. Players and coaches are often heard to say that they are taking things "one game at a time." They should go further and concentrate their energy on the most important components of performance when competing. For a pitcher, it could be throwing every pitch with thorough conviction. For a tennis player, it could be staying relaxed and fluid on every volley. For a golfer, it could be keeping the head down and following through on every single shot.

Take a minute now to rewrite your performance statement. Write down the one most important thing for you to think about as you prepare for competition. (Make sure that your performance statement does not include the word *don't* and that it is specific.)

____

____

____

____

____

____

Make a solemn promise to use your performance statement (or some other thought centered on enhancing performance or confidence) every time you catch yourself having negative thoughts. There is no need to beat yourself up if positive thinking isn't happening as often as you would like, but make it a point to keep working on it, and in time you will become better and better. Once you truly pledge to make your thoughts more beneficial, you will see that it is possible within even a few weeks to keep your inner dialogue more productive.

CHAPTER 3

The Personal Highlight Reel

Seeing Is Believing

Imagine what it must be like to wake up in the morning and turn on ESPN's "SportsCenter" to see highlights of yourself playing on national television. For some of my clients, this is a daily reality. As for the rest of us, we need to keep using our imaginations to experience this claim to fame. The personal highlight reel is an advanced form of visualization in which you create your own mental "SportsCenter" highlight reel.

The upside for the not-so-famous souls is that creating mental videos is actually more helpful than watching a video clip of one's success. There is an inherent benefit to generating the mental focus yourself: people learn faster by visualizing success rather than by watching it on tape. Of course, there is considerable value in watching success on tape. In fact, during film sessions, Bear Bryant, the famous football coach at Alabama, showed his players only footage of themselves playing well.

Coach Bryant contended that showing his players what they did well helped them repeat the performance, whereas showing them what they did wrong would only increase the likelihood of their exhibiting more poor play in the future.[1] Research backs up what Bryant suspected. It is much more helpful to have players think about success rather than failure. An asset of visualization is that by creating mental videos of success, the mind is more engaged than when merely watching a tape of previous success. Visualization helps athletes create a tighter focus on the variables needed for success.

A world-class, tae-kwon-do athlete with whom I work devised a personal highlight reel that included a sixty-second mental video of herself competing in the upcoming Olympic Trials and another sixty-second clip of herself competing in the 2008 Olympic Games and winning the gold medal. She uses her reel to accent her impressive power, speed, and strength. She watches it daily as part of her mental workout, and while doing so, she strives to feel the "relaxed confidence" that she wants to feel in competition. The more frequently she completes the personal highlight reel in her mental workouts, the more apt she is to use visualization during practices and competitions to perform at her best. Completing her mental workouts strengthens her mind to a point at which she's using visualization throughout training and competition to achieve the level of performance needed to make her Olympic dreams come true.

"Ty Is Back"

When I first met Tyler McIlwraith, she had just begun her senior basketball season at St. Louis University. Tyler had hopes of playing in the WNBA, but because of an early-season slump, she was beginning to wonder if a professional basketball career was realistic. Even her coaches had become concerned with her "nonaggressive" play. Although Tyler was trying, she was having trouble playing with the competitive fire that once came so naturally to her.

On offense, she was shooting more and more from the perimeter. Her shot was a little off because of a wrist injury, so she began passing up shots and giving the ball to her teammates rather than driving and creating offensive opportunities. Defensively, she had been moved into a new role because of an injury to a teammate. She felt awkward and uncertain in her new assignment, leaving her opponents one step ahead of her. All in all, Tyler was feeling less and less like the dominant player she was. She often thought about her mistakes and began questioning her ability to compete, which contributed to her being a less confident and aggressive player.

Fourteen games into her senior season, Tyler took up the 10-MT mental-training program. She began telling herself she was an aggressive, dominant player and replacing all self-doubt and negativity with mental images of herself as a dominant player playing with aggressiveness and intensity. Specifically, Tyler created a personal highlight reel that incorporated the following five scenarios:

Offensively

1. When an opponent comes from the help side, I jump-stop, draw contact, and then shoot. (The "help side" is the side of the court without the ball. A defender coming from the help side typically forms a double team. Tyler hoped to exploit the extra body defending her by drawing a foul call.)
2. When receiving a pass, I catch and immediately shoot. (No hesitation or stutter step.)

3. When I'm outside the three-point line with a player defending, I fake a shot and aggressively drive to the hoop. (Her goal is to create contact and, again, draw a foul.)

Defensively

1. When an opponent has the ball, I apply ball pressure in my stance with active hands.
2. When an opponent goes for the middle, I jump to her high foot and force her to the baseline. (In other words, Tyler wanted to use her body to cut off her opponent's angle to the basket or draw a charging foul.)

Every time Tyler would go through her mental workout, she would use her personal highlight reel to visualize herself performing the specified actions. Almost immediately, she started practicing with more determination and intensity. Her practice intensity began to carry into the games with her. Her coaches could not believe the turnaround.

One of Tyler's coaches had this to say about her improvements: "Ty is back. Whatever she is doing, it's working. It is somewhat unbelievable, but she is once again playing like we know she can. She is driving and scoring more; other teams are having to double up on her, and that is opening up more offensive opportunities for the whole team. She has really done a great job of leading this team."

Tyler finished her collegiate career stronger than ever. In addition to being named Practice Player of the Year and most valuable player of her team, Tyler was selected to the 2006–2007 ESPN the Magazine Academic All-American team and was named the Scholar-Athlete of the Year by the Division I-AAA Athletics Directors Association. With Tyler's work ethic and fresh mental approach to the game, she is well on her way to realizing her dreams of playing professional basketball. Tyler got herself on the right track by using her personal highlight reel to underscore the points of strength that help make her an intense and aggressive player. She cultivated a vision of what she could become by telling herself she was a dominant player and visualizing herself playing well on the basketball court.

User's Guide to Visualization

Research confirms that visualization is a powerful tool in athletics. According to some studies, in fact, every minute of visualization is worth seven minutes of physical practice.[2] I developed the personal highlight reel to help athletes more comprehensively focus on their individual control points for success. This tool is an advanced form of thought; it is a personalized video highlight clip that you visualize in your mind. Before creating your personal highlight reel, let's learn a few central aspects about visualizing.

Visualizing is the act of watching something in your mind before actually doing it. For example, if I wanted to shoot a free throw in basketball, I could close my eyes and see myself dribbling three times, lining up my sights on the back of the rim, and then shooting and making the free throw. I can actually feel what it is like to smoothly release the ball with just enough strength to have it soar through the air and hit nothing but net. I can hear the soft swish as the ball goes through the net and then the series of bounces until it comes to a rest.

There are eight essential guidelines for visualization success. The following sections explain each of the guidelines and give you an opportunity to practice before you assemble your own personal highlight reel.

Guideline 1: Choose One of Three Camera Angles

You can create your mental video from any of three "camera angles." Angle number one has you watching the mental video as if the camera is in the stands recording *someone other than you* performing the skill. This angle might feature someone who is exceptionally good at the skill you want to perform. In camera angle two, you are watching the mental video as if the camera is in the stands filming as *you* perform the skill. In camera angle three, you watch the mental video as if *your eyes are the camera* lens (or as if you're wearing a helmet camera). From this perspective, you would see whatever you actually see while you are performing the skill.

While visualization from any camera angle is helpful, angle number three is the most beneficial, because with this approach, your muscles can actually get stronger and **muscle memory** can develop. Many athletes refer to muscle memory as the ability to perform successfully while on autopilot. One of my clients had this to say on the subject: "When I am working on something, I mentally practice feeling it until I have muscle memory. Once I can feel it without trying, that's great, because I know it's time for me to pick something else to start improving."

Muscle memory: A successful sequence of muscle contractions that can be consistently repeated during athletic performance.

Research indicates that an athlete's muscles fire in sequence when the athlete visualizes from camera angle three. The mental image becomes a three-dimensional physical experience. It is normal for the individual initially to fluctuate between camera angles within the same mental video, but with practice, visualizing from camera angle number three becomes easier. Again, visualizing from any camera angle will aid you in making improvements, but angle three offers the added benefit of muscle memory.

Although I just told you that all three camera angles are helpful, I do not want you to use more than one camera angle when you visualize. Pick one angle to employ, trusting your instincts on which of the three is most appropriate for you.

Guideline 2: Pay Attention to Detail

The more detail you pack into your mental video, the more realistic and beneficial it is. Try to pay attention to three of the five senses while performing the skill: sight (What do you see on the surrounding field, court, or arena?); sound (Do you hear crowd noise, coaches, teammates?); and feel (What does the ball, bat, racket, club, etc., feel like? Also, what does your body feel like as it performs successfully?).

Guideline 3: Frequent and Brief Is the Ticket

Visualizing many times for short stints is far more effective than visualizing for extended periods. The ideal is to visualize one time before each physical turn taken. Thus, it is preferable to visualize once before each of three turns than to visualize three turns before performing all those turns uninterrupted. If your mind is focused and working prior to each physical turn taken, then every turn will be of increased quality. In some sports, such as golf, diving, and gymnastics, this is more realistic than with many traditional team sports such as basketball and football. Nevertheless, there are certain aspects of every sport that visualization can hone. The more often you complete your personal highlight reel in your mental workouts, the more inclined you will be to use short segments of visualization in training and competition just prior to performing. In addition, you will become better at using visualization to make improvements and increase consistency.

Guideline 4: Visualize from Beginning to End

Make sure to view the skill or action in its entirety. Creating a comprehensive mental video helps to reduce distraction and eliminate potential problems with emotional control. For example, you may tend to get nervous while warming up prior to competition. If you visualize yourself remaining calm and confident during warm-up and throughout the competition, you can improve your arousal control during the performance.

Also, be sure to pay attention to the desired result. For example, a basketball player wants to see herself going through her pre–free-throw routine, see the free throw, and then see the ball dropping smoothly through the net and landing on the floor.

Guideline 5: Emotionally Feel the Way You Want to Feel

Be aware of how you want to feel before and during competition, and then train yourself to feel just that way. For example, many athletes like to feel calm and confident prior to and during performances. Unfortunately, this state is not always easy to reach. Some athletes become overly excited or nervous during competition, while others feel underaroused or bored in certain situations. Both under- and overarousal can have ill effects on performance.

An arousal state is how energized or emotionally charged a person is at a given time. Often it is helpful for athletes to identify their ideal arousal state or what energy/emotional level helps them play at or beyond their potential. To identify your personal ideal arousal state, answer the following question. On a scale of 1 to 10 (where 1 is half asleep and 10 is running around 100 miles an hour), how "amped up" are you when you play your best? Take a moment and circle your ideal arousal state.

1 2 3 4 5 6 7 8 9 10

Athletes need to identify how they would like to feel prior to and during competition and then use visualization to accustom themselves to feel exactly that way in training as well as in competition. Take a moment to recall how you feel when you play your best. Drill down into that feeling, remembering that your emotions respond the same way your muscles do: the more you train them, the stronger they get. The more you mine a desired feeling, the more you teach yourself to feel that way in the future.

Guideline 6: Replay Until You Get It Right

Each time you use visualization, focus on what it takes for success as well as seeing the successful outcome. Perfection is not necessary for success. In 2006, the St. Louis Cardinals were World Series champions, but they were by no means perfect. Related to this point, the great golfer Ben Hogan wrote, "I stopped trying to do a great many difficult things perfectly because it had become clear in my mind that this ambitious over-thoroughness was neither possible nor advisable, or even necessary."[3]

If you have difficulty visualizing success at a given skill, pretend your mind is a DVD player: press Stop if an error occurs, rewind back to the beginning, and then press Replay. The mind can transcend physical limitations. Even if the body suffers setbacks in completing a skill successfully, the mind has the control to do so. Continue working on the skill mentally until success is achieved, and the body will follow suit.

Guideline 7: Give Credit Where Credit Is Due

Upon finishing each successful visualization, take a brief time-out to congratulate yourself on a job well done. A mental pat on the back or a few kind words to yourself after visualizing success will help keep you on an even keel. This simple gesture will have a positive impact on your self-image development as well as motivation. You will feel better about yourself and be more psyched to experience the successful attempt again.

Giving credit where due is both important and difficult. A lot of successful athletes are perfectionists in the sense that when they do well, they write it off as a personal expectation, and when they do poorly, they chastise themselves for their failures. Sports participation can be a humbling experience. If athletes do not learn to recognize when they have done something well, discouragement is inevitable.

Guideline 8: Operate at Game Speed

Finally, watch the mental clip at the desired speed. While it is helpful sometimes to slow the mental video down to figure out some of the more complex skills, you should always visualize at the desired speed prior to the physical performance, or else the timing of the action may be off. If your goal is in fact to increase the speed at which you are currently performing, see the increased speed in the mental video to raise the likelihood that it will happen.

When athletes think about pressure situations (competitions), they tend to visualize faster than the desired speed. As noted previously, it is common for stress to cause the heart rate to elevate and to accelerate the pace at which people perform. A mental video of a performance skill done at an elevated pace will tempt the player to physically rush the athletic performance, whereas visualizing at "game speed" will have a meaningful impact on improving performance.

Visualization Practice 1. Ready for some practice? Take a minute or so to picture yourself performing your chosen sport in a gamelike situation. See yourself performing well at game speed. Pay particular attention to feeling the way you want to feel in competition. See yourself warming up well and then performing well, and see the competition ending with the results you want. For instance, a defenseman on a professional hockey team might envision feeling strong during the morning skate, followed by playing a solid, physical game that night that results with his team winning. Note that it is important to see yourself as a winner. Experience what it takes to be successful and how it feels to perform at your best.

Now take a moment to write down some of the details:

What camera angle did you visualize from? ____________

What things did you see? ____________

What did you hear? ____________

What did you physically feel? ____________

Emotionally, what did it feel like to be successful? ____________

Did you give yourself credit for visualizing and performing well? ______

Visualization Practice 2. Take another sixty seconds and picture yourself in the biggest game situation you can imagine. See yourself in competition performing exactly the way you would want to perform in that situation. See yourself warming up well and performing well, and see the competition ending with the results you want. For example, that same hockey defenseman might visualize the morning skate before a Stanley Cup Finals game, in which he plays a key role later that night as his team comes away victorious. Be sure to emphasize yourself managing the pressure better than your competition. Make a mental note of the fact that you are more prepared for success in this situation than anyone else. Let yourself experience what it takes to be successful and how it feels to perform your best.

Once more, stop to write down some of the details you experienced:

Were you able to highlight yourself as the most prepared under pressure for success? ____________

What camera angle did you visualize from? ____________

What things did you see? ____

What did you hear? ____

What did you physically feel? ___________________________________

Emotionally, what did it feel like to be successful? _________________

Did you give yourself credit for visualizing and performing well? ______

Creating Your Personal Highlight Reel

Now that you know how to visualize, let's create your personal highlight reel. As you proceed, you may want to review the guidelines for visualization success. Pay special attention to visualizing from only one of the three camera angles, attempting to use the third camera angle whenever possible. Put energy into feeling the visualization both physically and emotionally, and conduct your visualizing at game speed.

The personal highlight reel is made up of three parts. The first part emphasizes a successful performance from your past, and the second and third parts address how you want to perform in the future.

Part 1: Sixty-Second Mental Video Clip of Excellent Past Performance

There are two options to consider when creating the first part of your personal highlight reel. The first option is to identify the best performance or game you have had in the past (the more recent the better). Imagine that the entire performance was videotaped; select three to five personal highlights from the videotaped performance, each lasting from ten to twenty seconds. The second option is to identify a few of your best performances and choose a combination of your best highlights from those performances. Choose the three to five best personal highlights, each lasting between ten to twenty seconds.

For either option, make sure you select a performance (or highlights) in which you felt great, played really well, and had a positive outcome. Arrange the highlights sequentially as they occurred and include as your last highlight the single greatest moment you have ever experienced in sport. To give you ideas for your content, the following is a representation of how part one of Scott Spiezio's personal highlight reel is structured.

Spiezio's Personal Highlight Reel (Part 1) of Successful Past Performance: 2006 NLCS—Game 2

- Game-saving triple to rally the team from behind and tie the game (the entire at bat)
- Ninth-inning double to drive in an insurance run (the entire at bat)
- Focused and intense in the field (two ground balls)
- Three-run home run in Game 6 of 2002 World Series (personal best moment in sport)

Notice that Scott chose the first option for part one of his personal highlight reel, recalling one great game from his past. For his single greatest moment in sport, Scott selected a recount of his famous 2002 World Series at bat, where he propelled his team to an eventual world championship. After Scott mentally recalls the 2002 World Series at bat, he turns his video into a freeze-frame photograph of himself crossing home plate, capturing his single greatest moment in a still frame. As he looks at himself in this mental photo, he turns up the intensity of how it felt and spends about ten seconds experiencing this positive emotion. In doing so, he influences his brain to release endorphins into his bloodstream, which are like powerful vitamins and minerals that enhance mood, motivation, and ability to deal with pain.

By visualizing a positive emotional experience from your past, you, too, can learn to release endorphins into your bloodstream on a regular basis, which is very helpful for increasing your confidence and consistency. You can just as easily adapt the imagery for business, personal fitness, or social situations in which you recapture the emotional sensation of giving a knockout presentation, or completing a solid run on a day you didn't even think you would make it to the gym, or even having the confidence to initiate a conversation with an attractive stranger.

List the three to five best performance highlights from your past along with your single greatest moment in sport. Be sure to turn your single greatest moment highlight video into a freeze-frame photo at the exact moment you experienced your greatest emotional rush. As you complete your mental workouts, turn up the intensity and really feel it—let the endorphins flow.

Your Successful Past Performance: ______________

- ______________________________
- ______________________________

▶ ____

▶ ____

▶ ____

Single greatest moment: ______________________________

Parts 2 and 3: Sixty-Second Mental Video Clips of Upcoming Big Games or Competitions

The second and third parts are also sixty-second mental video clips, but instead of re-creating the past, you imagine what you want to have happen in your future. The video clip for part two depicts chosen highlights of the next *upcoming* elevated-pressure game or event (similar to the previous exercise, in which you emphasized playing really well in a high-pressure situation), and part three spotlights the next scheduled game or practice for which you are preparing.

For part two, think of an upcoming important game, tryout, practice, or other event in which you will be participating. Imagine what you will need to do well to be successful. This is not necessarily the next time you compete, but the next high-stakes event. For example, if you are coming up on the postseason, the subject of this video clip might be the first playoff game even though it is still a week away.

As a sample template, here is a representation of how the second part of Spiezio's personal highlight reel might look as he anticipates returning to baseball. Note that its usefulness spans Division Series, League Championship Series, and World Series games:

Next Elevated-Pressure Game: Upcoming Postseason Game

- First at bat (thinking about seeing the ball and putting a short, compact swing on the ball)
- Second at bat (thinking about seeing the ball and putting a short, compact swing on the ball)
- Third at bat (thinking about seeing the ball and putting a short, compact swing on the ball)
- Fourth at bat (thinking about seeing the ball and putting a short, compact swing on the ball)
- Focused and intense, making two plays in the field (feeling relaxed and confident)

Adhering to the visualization guidelines, including always moving at the desired speed and feeling the way you most want to feel prior to and during the event, take a moment to create part two of your own personal highlight reel. See yourself doing well before and during the event. See yourself staying focused on what it takes to be successful, focusing on your performance statement and feeling your ideal arousal state. Also remember to see yourself as a winner and feel what it would feel like to perform well under pressure. Reminding yourself exactly how you want to feel and perform as you complete your personal highlight reel yields a big payoff.

Incorporate as much detail as you like. The rationale is to remind yourself of what you want to have happen in the future. The more energy you put into this, the more you improve your future prospects. Take a moment and fill in the specific details of part two of your personal highlight reel.

Your Next Elevated-Pressure Game: ______

- ______
- ______
- ______
- ______
- ______

The third and final sixty-second mental video clip features the next game or practice you are anticipating. As an example, here is how part three of Scott Spiezio's personal highlight reel could be constructed:

Next Regular-Season Game

- First at bat (thinking about seeing the ball and putting a short, compact swing on the ball)
- Second at bat (thinking about seeing the ball and putting a short, compact swing on the ball)
- Third at bat (thinking about seeing the ball and putting a short, compact swing on the ball)
- Fourth at bat (thinking about seeing the ball and putting a short, compact swing on the ball)
- Focused and intense, making two plays in the field (feeling relaxed and confident)

Notice that Spiezio's parts two and three are structured the same. However, the details included in the highlight reels would be different, because the game, opponent, atmosphere, and pitcher would likely change. For instance, his team might be playing against the Red Sox in Boston during the World Series in part two of the reel, which covers the prospective next big game on the schedule. The pitcher starting for the Sox could be a veteran flamethrower with a ninety-seven-mile-per-hour fastball like Josh Beckett. Part three of Scott's reel may be a late-September home game against a division opponent, who is starting a rookie pitcher with mostly off-speed breaking balls.

Time to generate part three of your personal highlight reel. Piece together a sixty-second video clip wherein you see yourself warming up well and then performing well in your next practice and/or game. See yourself holding your focus steady (performance statement) and feeling emotionally (ideal arousal state) and physically the way you want to feel during the performance. Definitely see yourself as a winner and feel what it would feel like to perform well under pressure. Your part three may resemble or be exactly the same as what you envision for part two. Nevertheless, it is important to go over part three in detail because here, you are picturing yourself in a different atmosphere.

Your Next Game: ______________________________

- ______________________________
- ______________________________
- ______________________________
- ______________________________
- ______________________________

Personal Highlight Examples

To close out this chapter, let's put it all together. There are three parts to your personal highlight reel, with each part containing three to five specific highlights lasting approximately sixty seconds. Part one is either a recount of one great performance from your past (option one) or a combination of highlights from several of your great performances (option two) and a recollection of your single greatest moment in sport. Part two of your personal highlight reel focuses specifically on how you want to perform in an upcoming competition of elevated importance; part three focuses on the details of how you want to perform in the next scheduled competition. Be sure to really hone in on what it physically feels like to emphasize your performance statement and emotionally focus on your ideal arousal state as you go through parts two and three of your personal highlight reel. By doing so, you will dramatically increase the effectiveness of your visualization.

Following are two full-length examples of how personal highlight reels unfold. The first is Sean Townsend's, and the second is Tyler McIlwraith's. Notice that both Sean and Tyler keep their focus simple and concrete. At the end of Chapter 5 you will transfer the details of your personal highlight reel to your Mental Workout Work Sheet.

Sean Townsend's Personal Highlight Reel

Part 1 (Successful Past Performance): World Championships '02

- Good training leading up to World Championships
- Felt calm and confident in warm-ups; everything was smooth and fluid

- Hit four solid routines on the first day of competition
- Superhit P-bars to win the gold
- Personal greatest moment in sport: gold medal ceremony (freeze frame: standing at the top of the podium)

Part 2 (Next Elevated-Pressure Competition): USA Championships '08

- Good, solid warm-up, feeling calm and confident and taking one skill at a time, one routine at a time
- Hit all six routines on day one while feeling calm and confident and taking one skill at a time, one routine at a time
- Hit all six routines in finals while feeling calm and confident and taking one skill at a time, one routine at a time

Part 3 (Next Competition): WOGA Invitational

- Good, solid warm-up, feeling calm and confident and taking one skill at a time, one routine at a time
- Hit all six routines on day one while feeling calm and confident and taking one skill at a time, one routine at a time
- Hit all six routines in finals while feeling calm and confident and taking one skill at a time, one routine at a time

Tyler McIlwraith's Personal Highlight Reel

Part 1 (Successful Past Performance): SLU vs. Arkansas

- Good warm-up, feeling relaxed and confident
- Playing aggressively on offense, calling for the ball and being very vocal with teammates

- Creating offense with good moves and shot selection
- Playing strong defense, continually moving my feet and hands
- Rebounding on both sides of the ball, strong and aggressive
- Personal greatest moment in sport: beating University of Richmond to qualify for conference tournament (freeze frame: celebrating in the locker room after the game)

Part 2 (Next Elevated-Pressure Game): Conference Championship Game

- Aggressive play for all forty minutes of the game: start strong, strong in the middle, finish strong
- Offensively driving hard to the basket and going after contact
- Defensively keep my feet moving and have active hands
- Pay attention to being extremely vocal with my teammates, calling defenses, and calling for the ball

Part 3 (Next Game): Next Regular-Season Game

- Aggressive play for all forty minutes of the game: start strong, strong in the middle, finish strong
- Offensively driving hard to the basket and going after contact
- Defensively keep my feet moving and have active hands
- Pay attention to being extremely vocal with my teammates, calling defenses, and calling for the ball

CHAPTER 4

The Identity Statement

Influencing Self-Image

An identity statement is a self-statement designed to improve **self-image**. Your self-image is essentially how you view yourself—what strengths and weaknesses you believe you possess. It has been demonstrated that what people believe they are capable of accomplishing largely determines how much they will actually accomplish. Self-image is a proven agent of behavior control. When you truly believe in your ability, the self-image motivates the behaviors needed for you to live up to your expectations.

Self-image: The level of success a person believes he or she is capable of achieving.

The effect of self-image is one reason why 80 percent of lottery winners file for bankruptcy within five years of winning. Even though their financial situation has dramatically changed, typically the self-image hasn't. For people who see themselves as not good with money, no matter how much money is given to them, they will generally find a way to lose it. Along those same lines, on February 10, 2008, the Clemson basketball team took the court to try to break a string of fifty-three losses in a row to the ever powerful University of North Carolina squad. Clemson dominated the entire game and led by sixteen points with less than eight minutes remaining, only to go on and lose the game by ten points. After being defeated for a heartbreaking fifty-fourth consecutive time, the Clemson team continues to host a self-image issue when it comes to playing the UNC Tar Heels.

The Walk-In Runner

Even from the first time Jenny (whose name I've changed for confidentiality purposes) showed up in the waiting room of my office in February 2000, I knew that her situation was serious. It was two days after I had given a lecture about drugs and alcohol for a school district in St. Louis. She was a fifteen-year-old freshman and had been in the audience for what she referred to as my "drug talk." She was tall and thin, with long, straight hair, baggy jeans, flip-flops, and a long-sleeved T-shirt with the word *Yes* printed on it. Her hair and clothes were dirty, she wore no makeup, her eyes were red, and her skin was pale and blotchy. She looked rough, scared, and lonely.

Jenny didn't have an appointment, but I could tell something urgent brought her to my office that day, and she looked determined. When I asked her if she could come back in a couple of hours, she bluntly replied, "I'll wait."

During that period, Jenny was smoking marijuana every day—or at least every day she could get her hands on it. She had never met her father and hadn't seen her mother in more than five years. She lived with an aunt most of the time, and she was flunking every class except gym.

Jenny was scared, and she needed help. She wanted to do better in school, and she wanted stop doing drugs, but she didn't know how. I agreed to try to help her if she would agree to a couple of things: First, she had to start going to school every day; and second, she had to come see me once a week. I told her if she was late or missed even one session, I would not be able to help her. She did well for about a month, and then she didn't show up for one of our meetings. I assumed she had given up and gone back to her old ways. The next morning, I received a phone call from her aunt. Jenny had overdosed at a concert the night before and ended up in the hospital. A security guard had summoned an ambulance after he found Jenny unconscious on the floor of the bathroom.

Jenny's aunt asked if I would continue to try to help her niece, and I agreed to see Jenny the next week. To my surprise, when she showed up, she looked better than I had ever seen her. Her eyes looked sad but not as red or lonely.

She asked me for a favor: "Will you help me get on the track team?"

Jenny's grades were too poor for her to officially join the team, but the coach allowed her to come to practice and said that she could formally join the team if her grades improved sufficiently. After a couple of weeks, the track coach called me and reported that Jenny was a pretty decent runner. She started making it to school, practice, and our weekly meetings regularly. Her grades didn't improve enough the first season for her to qualify for the team, but by the next season, they were high enough that she was eligible to compete.

I continued to see Jenny for the better part of the next two years, but it was her track coach who really helped her. Jenny was a strong runner, and the coach pushed her to get her grades up. Over and over, he told her that she was a good runner and that she was smart enough to get good grades. Before long, she started internalizing what her coach was telling her. She started to believe in her ability to run, and she knew she could do better in her classes. She ended up graduating from high school with a 2.6 grade point average, and she received a scholarship to run track at a junior college. She eventually went on to make the track team at a Division I university and graduated with a 3.0 grade point average.

She is now a teacher and assistant track coach at a prominent high school in Oklahoma. When I first met Jenny, she told me she was stupid and she wasn't good at anything. Now she will tell you she can do anything if she puts her mind to it. Her self-image changed, and that is what allowed her to change her life.

Self-image is internally constructed: we can decide how we view ourselves. The experience I had with Jenny taught me very early the powerful impact of maintaining a positive self-image. Each of us chooses how we see ourselves. Creating and using a positive identity statement will help you choose a powerful self-image.

Who Are You and What Do You Want?

This choice of how you view yourself is the essence of the identity statement, the fourth tool in the mental workout. The identity statement is similar to the performance statement; it is a statement you can use to increase ability and develop a potent self-image.

As pointed out previously, largely what determines people's self-image is the things they continually say to themselves, and unfortunately, much of our inner dialogue regards what we can't do rather than what we can do. Simply put, the individual who steps up to the starting line with a true belief in his or her ability to do well has a much greater likelihood of success than those who don't have that mind-set.

You can't outperform or underperform your self-image for long. The self-image will eventually regulate behaviors and outcomes to fall within the range of self-expectation. Essentially, your self-image governs how successful you will become. If you truly believe in your capacity to triumph, then you will manage to make it happen. Conversely, if your self-image is low, you will unfortunately come up short of your potential no matter how hard you try.

In 2007, Zach Johnson came out of virtually nowhere to beat the great Tiger Woods in one of the most memorable Masters Championships in history. The young man from Iowa took the country by storm with his ferocious competitiveness on the course. Off the course, Johnson endeared himself to golf fans with his genuine sense of humility. In a postvictory interview, he stated, "I'm Zach Johnson and I'm from Cedar Rapids, Iowa. I'm a normal guy."[1]

He also said of himself, "I don't hit it far, I can't overpower a course, but I think I am mentally tough."[2] He asserted, "Competition in general is just in my skin. It's always been there. I really don't care what it is; it can be the most subtle thing. I want to win."[3]

Zach Johnson is not a client of mine, but when I read this quote of his, it confirmed the importance of self-image. Johnson started the final round of the 2007 Masters Championship two shots out of the lead and one shot behind Woods. He leaned on his competitive nature, mental toughness, and true belief in himself to overcome the odds and surge to a David-conquers-Goliath type of victory over Woods and the rest of the pack.

Self-Image Management Is the Answer

In a revised version of Dr. Maxwell Maltz's work *Psycho-Cybernetics,* testimonies from top athletes such as Jack Nicklaus and Payne Stewart and coaches such as Pat Riley and Phil Jackson support Maltz's position regarding the powerful impact that self-image has on athletic performance.[4] Self-image is not mental trickery; it is a scientifically proven agent of control. The self-image identifies and motivates the necessary behavior and connects it to the desired outcome. The key is to create the self-image desired—decide who you want to be and how you want to live—and then continuously tell yourself that you have what it takes to be that person. The self-image will guide and direct actions and behaviors until the self-image becomes the reality.

In the words of Maxwell Maltz, "You will act like the sort of person you conceive yourself to be. More important, you literally cannot act otherwise, in spite of all your conscious efforts or willpower. This is why trying to achieve something difficult with teeth gritted is a losing battle. Willpower is not the answer. Self-image management is."

Self-image management begins by deciding to believe in yourself and your ability to accomplish great things. For

Jenny, the powerful component of self-image influenced her work ethic. Her revamped self-image helped her work through tough times. Most important, she used her identity statement to chase away her negative thoughts and self-doubt. She stopped thinking about what she couldn't do and started thinking about what she wanted to do. She believed in herself and committed to finding a way to stop using drugs, graduate from high school, and eventually become successful as a teacher and coach. Jenny's identity statement, "I am smart and capable. I am able to do anything when I put my mind to it," gave her something positive to think about instead of self-doubt. It helped her call forth the courage needed to go out and lay claim to her dreams.

Creating Your Identity Statement

I encourage athletes to create a two-part identity statement. The first part indicates a strength you currently have or want to have. Be sure the strength you choose to accentuate makes achieving success more likely. For example, your strength might be that you are a really hard worker. Whether it is already true or is something that you want to be true, the first part of your identity statement might be "I am the hardest worker on the team."

The second part of your identity statement addresses what you want to accomplish. It is OK to stretch a bit here. According to research on affirmations, the more imposing the desired task, the more impact it will have on the self-image. Frame both parts of your identity statement as though the objectives have already been achieved. In this way, you own your self-image in the here and now. A straightforward way to do this is to start each half of your identity statement with "I am . . ." Remember what we know about self-image: you cannot achieve your goals and dreams until your current self-image reflects your ability to do so.

My own personal identity statement is "I am more motivated than my competition; I am the most effective sport psychology consultant in the world." When I say, "I am more motivated than my competition," that mostly means that I will outwork any of my peers and that I will always find a way to help my clients. I love what I do, I love to help people, and I am 100 percent committed to doing whatever it takes to help my clients reach their goals. I believe that the level of care I provide is directly related to my goal of reaching supreme effectiveness.

When I say, "I am more motivated" and "I am the most effective sport psychology consultant in the world," I am obliging myself to draw a bead on how I want things to be. By pointing myself toward how I want reality to be, I impel myself to do whatever is needed to make it come about. Once you create your identity statement, commit to using it. Completing your mental workout daily will be invaluable in this regard, and if you repeat your identity statement every time you catch yourself having thoughts of negativity or self-doubt, eventually your self-image will begin to shape the reality you desire. This is hard work, but it *is* doable.

To create your identity statement, answer the following questions:

1. What is the foremost strength you possess (or want to possess) that proves you can achieve greatness? (Example: "I am more motivated than my competition.")

____

____

2. What do you ultimately hope to accomplish in your sport? (Example: "I am the most effective sport psychology consultant in the world.")

____

____

3. Put both parts together, assuring that you use the present tense. (Example: "I am more motivated than my competition; I am the most effective sport psychology consultant in the world.") This is your identity statement.

____

____

Examples of Identity Statements

- **Baseball.** I am the hardest worker on the team; I am a dominant major-league hitter.
- **Basketball.** I am intelligent and I know this game better than anyone; I am the most prolific scorer on the court.
- **Football.** I am fast and strong; I am the most powerful running back in the league.
- **Golf.** I am more mentally and physically prepared than my competition; I am a dominant professional golfer.
- **Gymnastics.** I am a hard worker, and I have what it takes; I am a world-class gymnast.
- **Wrestling.** I am talented, and I work hard; I am unstoppable in competition.

CHAPTER 5

Another Centering Breath and Away We Go . . .

At midnight (CST) in St. Louis, my phone rang. It was one of my clients, a college baseball player who lives in Phoenix, Arizona.

"What time is it there?" he asked.

"Midnight." I responded.

"Is it too late to talk?" he asked.

"Yes," I said, wiping the sleep away. "I am awake now. What is the problem?"

"No problem," he said. "I just wanted to let you know I figured out what I was doing wrong."

The person on the other end of the phone was Mike Beal, a talented third baseman with an unrelenting work ethic. Mike has a fervent desire to play professional baseball and has the makeup to do so. He is coordinated, strong, and smart, and he works diligently at improving his game. Mike had been in a brief hitting slump prior to calling me that evening. He is as physically and mentally prepared as any athlete I have ever counseled. He goes all out in practice and devotes extra time to working on his hitting and foot speed, and he always completes his mental workout before practices and games.

Nevertheless, Mike was not having his customary quality at bats in games. He was getting out in front on his swings. (As referenced in Chapter 1, being "out in front" means the hitter is starting the swing too early and shifting his weight from the back foot to the front foot too soon, which usually produces a weak swing.)

Mike had been going through his mental workouts prior to games just as he had been instructed, which got him excited and ready to play. The problem was that he was doing a halfhearted centering breath to start the mental workout and forgetting altogether to do a final centering breath at the conclusion. Mike figured out that not doing a good centering breath to start his mental workout was causing him to speed up his visualization a bit. In essence, he was visualizing himself hitting off pitchers throwing somewhere between ninety and ninety-three miles per hour when in reality the pitchers he was facing were throwing between eighty-two and eighty-five miles per hour.

Mike was out in front on his swing because he had been visualizing the need for a faster reaction. He also realized that by not finishing the mental workout with a good centering breath, he was entering the games a "little too jacked up." Mike recognizes that he plays his best when he is feeling calm and confident. When he does his mental workout, he feels "excited and confident," and that is why his final centering breath is paramount. It is essential for athletes to know how to keep themselves calm and relaxed prior to competition.

Mike was so delighted that he had ascertained what needed to change that he just had to call me after the game to share the news. He actually went 0 for 3 that night, but in thinking about how to correct what went wrong afterward, he remembered the importance of using both centering breaths. As advertised, after he started using the centering breaths, he began having more patient, quality at bats. He was staying back longer and started hitting with power again.

Once More with Feeling

Remember: the centering breath is a deep breath used to physiologically control heart rate and arousal. Taking a centering breath at the end of the mental workout is necessary for athletes because completing the personal highlight reel may cause the heart rate and arousal state to elevate. You always want to feel calm, confident, and relaxed up to the point of competition. The final centering breath helps control arousal and conserve energy needed for training and competition.

Kay Porter, a well-known sport psychologist, talks in her book *The Mental Athlete* about the potential overuse of visualization and mental work.[1] She gives examples of athletes who have actually tired themselves out from doing too much mental work prior to training and competition. So, it is possible to overdue mental work. I tell athletes that doing the mental workout one time a day is great. Some clients prefer to do it a couple of times a day, and that is OK, but there is no need to do it more than twice a day.

I often encourage athletes to skip the mental workout if it feels like "work." Taking a day off is preferable to completing the mental work with low intensity. Your body listens to what your brain tells it, and if your brain is telling it to train and compete with less than 100 percent intensity, then your body will conform. My experience has been that athletes enjoy doing their mental workouts. The 10-MT mental workout is short enough that it should leave you feeling energized rather than worn down.

The 10-MT workout is designed to help athletes control arousal (through centering breaths), create a precise and effective focus (through the performance statement and personal highlight reel), and improve self-image (through the identity statement). The mental workout is a vehicle for learning and making appropriate corrections. If athletes use the mental workout correctly, it helps them target the learning of new skills more quickly and improve existing skills more efficiently.

Mike Beal uses his centering breaths to control his heart rate and arousal after he envisions his personal highlight reel, which often stimulates the body physiologically. In this way, he is able to emphasize a patient swing in which he keeps his weight back longer. Athletes typically find that as they commit to doing their mental workouts, they also begin using the tools throughout practices and games.

For example, when Mike is on deck, he finds himself taking a centering breath and visualizing and feeling a top-quality swing. He fixes his brain on relaxing and staying back just before he steps into the batter's box, which appreciably increases his likelihood of having a quality at bat. I can attest that the tools in the mental workout help every athlete do this in some form or another. Using the mental workouts consistently helps ensure that the mind is focused enough to know what to think and strong enough to maintain that focus during competition.

The last centering breath is the cooldown stage of your 10-MT workout. Aerobic exercise classes, Pilates classes, and the like, usually conclude with some sort of cooldown stretching exercises. Likewise, distance runners are sure to stretch their hamstrings, quadriceps, and other leg muscles to minimize soreness as their muscles cool off. With your mental workout, the final centering breath serves a similar purpose. It brings your exercise full circle and ensures that your heart rate is at the proper level.

Phase 1 Review

Let's take this opportunity to review the five tools in the mental workout before we move forward.

First is the centering breath, which will take you fifteen seconds. Then you recite to yourself your performance statement, a self-statement designed to improve your focus on what it takes (process of success) to be successful; this should take about five seconds. In the third step, you run through your personal highlight reel, comprising three sixty-second clips of visualizations, for three minutes total. When your personal highlight reel is over, you deliver to yourself your identity statement, a self-statement to help you focus on developing the self-image you desire; as with the performance statement, this will take five seconds. You finish the mental workout with another fifteen-second centering breath.

All told, the entire mental workout will take up approximately three minutes and forty seconds of your time. I hereby challenge you, immediately, to start arriving at practice a little early so you can properly execute your mental workout.

A considerable body of research validates that each of these five tools is highly effective for improving an individual's ability to perform. What I have done is to organize and structure the tools into a simple and concrete mental workout. Once you have learned how to manipulate these tools, you can apply them to every facet of your life that demands a little toughness.

The thousands of athletes, business executives, and personal clients with whom I have worked have taught me that formatting the tools in this way allows for the true development of mental toughness. Give it a try. Complete the mental workout for two weeks, and judge for yourself if it helps you to improve focus, ability, and consistency.

If you will commit to completing your mental workouts as part of your everyday training, you will begin to acquire the mental toughness needed to unlock previously hidden potential. Once you do, you are apt to start using bits and pieces of your mental workout throughout practices and competition. Wielding the various tools in practices and competition will also help to increase your consistency and quality of work.

PHASE 2

GOAL SETTING FOR GREATNESS

CHAPTER 6

Effective Goal Setting

Creating and Achieving the Dream

The second phase of the 10-Minute Toughness mental-training plan is the identification and achievement of goals. I believe the 10-MT goals program is the finest program of its type. I know from personal experience that when it is time to talk about goals, many people gloss over the subject. I hope you will read these next three chapters with an open mind. I have made an effort to create an easy-to-complete program that can bring solid results on a *daily* basis.

This chapter explains the three levels of goals and how to avoid the common pitfalls in effective goal setting. Chapter 7 then shows you how to use incentives and vision integrity to enhance motivation. In Chapter 8, whose topic is work ethic, you get a practical resource for being more physically and mentally prepared than your competition.

After reviewing the sample work sheets provided, including Goal Setting for Greatness, you can turn to Appendix B for blank forms to complete on your own.

When it comes to goals, I believe three main concepts are of the utmost importance, yet they are often overlooked in the goal-setting process. The three concepts that turn ordinary goal setting into effective goal setting are these:

1. Process goals produce results
2. No excuses; go public
3. Keep goals alive, and live the dream

The following sections plumb these three concepts and explain how to apply them to your life to further improve on mental toughness and preparation for success.

Process Goals Produce Results

With his team leading 5–2 in the top of the sixth inning, a young minor-league pitcher whom we will call Steve was all too aware that if he could get through this inning, not only would he lower his ERA, but also he might get a much needed win. (ERA—earned run average—as noted in Chapter 2, reflects the average number of runs allowed per nine innings.) He kept thinking about how urgently he needed to lower his ERA if he was ever going to make it to the big leagues. All year, he had worried about how many runs he was allowing, and he knew that his ERA, which was now more than 4.5, was too high to carry him to the majors. It seemed as if the more tightly he focused on lowering his ERA, the higher it got.

Since it was already late in the season, he knew he needed to start stringing some solid outings together if he was going to finish the year with his ERA under 4.0. As the first hitter of the inning stepped in, the pitcher was preoccupied with not letting another runner cross the plate. He said to himself, "If I can just get through this inning, they will probably lift me, which will keep me in line for the victory, and my ERA would be only 3.0 for the day. I can do this. Just get through this inning."

The batter hit a line drive off the wall that ended up as a long single. With one man on and no outs, again Steve began obsessing about his ERA. The next batter hit a line drive to the third baseman, and the runner at first was thrown out for a double play. "One more out; all I need is one more out. I can do this," the pitcher told himself. The third hitter walked on four straight balls. After another single, the opposing team had men on first and third with two outs. Steve again was reduced to musings about statistics and the likelihood of his major-league dream slipping away. The next man up hit a long fly ball to the outfield that was reeled in by the left fielder. The pitcher got out of the inning, and his team wound up winning the game. Although Steve commented in our next meeting that he was pleased with the outing and getting the win, I could not help thinking that he had lost more than he had won.

Paradox of the Product Goal

Steve's way of thinking is an all-too-common mistake that athletes make with goals. I call this the *paradox of the product goal.* The paradox of the product goal is that the more you think about your product goals in competition, the further you are from achieving them. The mistake Steve made was that during the game, he let his mind dwell on the product goals he had set at the beginning of the season. Product goals are result-oriented goals that people set for themselves. Steve's primary product goals were to have an ERA of 3.5 or less and to win sixteen or more games. Both of these goals are outcome oriented and are pretty good goals to have. Setting product goals isn't the problem; in fact, I highly recommend using product goals. However, athletes must learn when to promote product goals and when it is more appropriate to concentrate on their process goals. A simple guideline is to use product goals *before* and *after* practices and competitions, and to use process goals *during* practices and competitions.

Steve doesn't pitch better when he thinks about his ERA. As a matter of fact, thinking about ERA while pitching actually impedes his ability to pitch well. Steve would gain ground from thinking about his process goals, or what it takes to have a low ERA. He could have been occupied with keeping his weight back and his arm on top, so as to keep the ball down in the strike zone. ("Weight back, arm on top, down in the zone" is also Steve's performance statement.) Even though Steve was successful for the day in lowering his ERA and getting his team a crunch-time win, he did not help himself for his next outing. The next time he pitched, he again focused on his statistics, and he left half of the pitches he threw up in the strike zone. When Steve instead keeps his mind on his process goals (what it takes to have a low ERA), he is able to pitch with much better success.

Steve and I trotted out to the practice field with a ball and glove one day to conduct an experiment. For the first ten pitches, I had Steve think right before he started his windup about how nice it would be to have an

ERA lower than 3.5. After each pitch, I asked him if he placed the ball down in the strike zone where he wanted it. Of those ten pitches, only three were down enough in the zone, according to Steve. For the next ten pitches, I asked Steve to think about "weight back, arm on top" just prior to pitching. For this set, he said that he was able to command six out of ten down in the zone where he wanted them.

In time, Steve learned to get command on eight out of every ten pitches, by training his mind to think only about the process goals, or what it takes to be successful, rather than thinking about the success itself. I repeat: thinking about the success is of value, but do it before and after practice and competition, not during the performance. I advised Steve to think about his targeted low ERA in the evenings to motivate him to get a good night's sleep and his desired sixteen wins in the morning when the alarm went off to get out of bed and get in a full day of training. Let your desire for success motivate you to make good decisions about healthy living and effective training.

A Cy Young Award–winning pitcher once told me that one of his best outings was in a crucial playoff game in which he surrendered a late-inning game-winning home run. He said that while he was obviously disappointed that his team lost, he recognized that he had stayed focused on his keys for success throughout the game. He kept the ball down in the strike zone, and he worked the inside and outside of the plate while changing speeds. Even though he came out on the losing end, he pitched his game, and he knew that by staying focused on his *process of success,* he would undoubtedly win more games than he would lose. He was right on: he eventually led his team to a World Series victory.

Ultimate goal: The culmination of what you want to accomplish and how you want to accomplish it.

Three Levels of Goals

The 10-Minute Toughness mental workout is optimized when athletes know how to set effective goals for themselves. The three levels, or types, of goals that I discuss with clients are **ultimate goals**, product goals, and process goals (the latter two were previewed in the Introduction). The work an athlete does to meet these three levels of goals unlocks hidden potential, increases motivation, creates pinpoint focus, and reenergizes training and competition.

- **Ultimate goals.** Ultimate goals are the culmination of what you want to accomplish and how you want to accomplish it. When identifying your ultimate goals, imagine being able to look into the future and witness your retirement dinner. What accomplishments do you want to hang on the wall, and what would you like the speaker to say about you regarding how you played the game and how you conducted yourself?
- **Product goals.** Product goals are result-oriented goals. They are clearly measurable and usually are most effective if they emphasize accomplishments in the next twelve months. I have found that the best formula is to assign yourself up to three product goals for the next competitive season in which you will participate and, again, up to three product goals for the upcoming off-season. For example, a basketball player may have the following three product goals for the season:

  1. Score at least ten points per game
  2. Have a free-throw percentage of 80 percent or better
  3. Grab at least six rebounds every game

- **Process goals.** Process goals are the "what it takes" to achieve the product goals you set. Process goals also must be specific enough to be measurable. For example, the same basketball player may believe that two of the best ways for her to score ten points per game are by being mentally prepared for each game and by aggressively driving to the hoop (within five feet) at least four times per game. "Being mentally prepared" is tricky to measure; however, the basketball player could substitute, "I want to complete my mental workout every day prior to practices and games." Doing the mental workouts consistently will certainly contribute to her being mentally prepared. Each completed mental workout is a valid measure of mental preparedness. Similarly, by defining the aggressive drive to the hoop as a drive that gets her within five feet of the basket, she makes the goal readily measurable.

It's understandable for athletes to care more about their product goals, because these traditionally are the statistical standards of success for comparing athletes. While setting specific statistical goals for a given season can be a useful motivational tool, it can also be counterproductive for producing results, as in Steve's case. Athletes need to learn how to shift their thinking from results to the process required to notch those results.

Although results count, the healthiest and most reliable method of producing positive results is to prioritize the process of success as it pertains to individual behavior. An optimal way to train your mind to stay focused on your process of success is to emphasize it in your mental workouts. As you complete your mental workouts, see yourself zeroing in on the process goals that impel you to perform at your best, especially as you review your personal highlight reel and performance statement. By visualizing yourself maintaining the mental focus, you are better able to call it forth in competition.

No Excuses; Go Public

It is important to write your goals down and let others know of your intentions. The act of writing down as well as talking about your goals makes them more a part of your reality. The more you can see and recite your goals, the more steadily they move from your subconscious into your awareness. Writing and talking about your goals will also increase your accountability and motivation for achieving them. A client of mine had this to say after qualifying to compete in the Track and Field World Championships: "I had to make it to Worlds. I told everyone I knew that I was going to make it; that alone made me work harder, because I didn't want to let myself or anyone else down."

In Chapter 8, I will ask you to spend a couple of minutes writing your goals down. I also urge you to talk about them with other people. Let others know what your goals are, and then use the accountability that results to more fully commit to achieving your greatest aspirations. I have worked with a certain football player for more than four years. When I first met him, he was going into his senior year of high school, and he was reputed to be one of the top linebackers in the St. Louis area. When he came into my office, I was surprised, because he seemed to be undersized. It took only a few minutes with this young man for me to realize how it was that size—or speed, for that matter—wouldn't slow him down. When I asked him if he was big enough to play at the next level, his response was, "Do you know what Coach John Wooden says about excuses?" Although I am familiar with the famous UCLA basketball coach and his work, I played along: "What does Coach Wooden say about excuses?" He replied, "Never make excuses. Your friends won't need them, and your foes won't believe them."

Although this young man was not remarkably big, strong, or fast, he more than made up for his deficiency through attitude and accountability. He refused to make excuses, because, he said, "excuses stop me from getting better." Even though making excuses is normal, Coach Wooden and this young football player know whereof they speak. Excuses promote underachieving. If you have an excuse (even if it's a good one) for falling short of your goals, you render it much more probable that you will continue to achieve less. If, instead, you adopt a no-excuses approach, you will nurture the accountability needed for eventually accomplishing your goals.

That football player is a perfect example of the power of never using excuses. Although he was twenty pounds small for his position and not especially fast, he worked hard enough to earn a Division I partial scholarship and is currently a cocaptain of his team. He has a new goal of playing professional football, and knowing him, I'm sure he will find a way to make it happen.

I encourage every client I have to adopt the no-excuses mentality. I also prod my clients to go public about not making excuses. Telling others about the no-excuses mentality reinforces your likelihood of eschewing excuses in your life. Every time you talk to someone about not accepting excuses, you imprint the no-excuses mentality on your conscious mind.

Talking about something makes it more real. Going public with your goals and your no-excuses approach to them makes you more apt to put the needed energy into overcoming obstacles and achieving your goals, even those you may initially fall short of reaching. By letting other people know your intentions, you exert a little more pressure on yourself to be accountable. I believe that accountability is one of the most positive character traits a person can possess. If you hold yourself accountable to reaching your expectations, you position yourself to ultimately bask in the glory of success.

Keep Goals Alive, and Live the Dream

As I stated earlier, most coaches and athletes look at goals only a couple of times per season. This is not an effective use of goals. For goals to work, they must become a part of daily training. I said this to a Division I basketball coach, and he looked at me as though I was crazy. He asked me facetiously, "What are you talking about? Do you think we have time to take our personal goal sheets out to practice with us every day? Are we supposed to look at our goals before every drill, or would you prefer we chant these goals as we run sprints?" I responded with a straight face, "Yes, Coach, I think that is exactly what you should do, and then you could all hold hands and sing songs around the campfire." Thankful that he laughed at my joke, I proceeded to ask him a few questions about how he was currently using goals.

"When you are out there at practice," I asked, "does every coach have a clear idea of exactly what you are trying to improve?" He answered dryly, "Yes, they do, or they won't be on the staff for long." I then asked, "How about every player?" Again he responded without emotion: "They better." I knew I would get his attention with the next question: "What if I were to tell you that when

I spoke with some of the players, very few could actually tell me what specifically they were trying to improve?" The coach looked at me as though he were about to make me run sprints. Their answers included, "We're just trying to get better" and "We do the drills to make the coaches happy." The real problem is that this posture is often the norm: most athletes don't take full advantage of the power of goals.

In fact, Stephen Covey[1] reported in his book *The 8th Habit* that only 37 percent of individuals have a clear understanding of what their team is trying to achieve and why they are trying to achieve it, and only 20 percent are enthusiastic about the organization's goals. Covey's findings indicate that only four of the eleven members of a basketball team know the team's keys for success, and only two of the eleven really care about it (and those numbers include coaches).

I don't think athletes need to carry their goal sheets around during practice, but athletes and coaches alike will benefit considerably from spending a couple of minutes prior to practice identifying exactly what it is they want to improve that day. Goals must be utilized for them to work—and the more often, the better. Let's try a little experiment:

1. Write down one specific thing that you as an athlete or coach would like to improve in your next practice or game.

   ____

2. Now write down one thing you can do differently in your next practice or game that could help you make the improvement you just named.

   ____

If you devoted any amount of time and energy into answering those two questions, you have just put the power of goal setting to work for yourself. By thinking in terms of what you want and exactly how you can get what you want, you pull your goal closer within reach. Many of us get caught up in life, and we often go through the motions of practice without having specific and clear targets for what we want to improve.

The goal-setting portion of 10-MT helps athletes bring their goals to life by setting and using goals every day in practice. I promise that it is simple and straightforward and will take only an additional three to four minutes per day.

The 10-MT goal-setting plan is a three-step process:

1. Further on in this book, you will take a few minutes to write down your ultimate goals. Remember that ultimate goals are the summary accomplishments you want from your sport and how you want to be remembered as going about achieving those accomplishments. Additionally, you will set two product goals for the upcoming season, including three process goals needed to help achieve each of the product goals.
2. After practices and games, you will take about three to four minutes to fill out a Success Log. The Success Logs ask athletes to answer the following questions:

    - What three things did I do well today?
    - Based on today's performance, what do I want to improve?
    - What is one thing I can do differently that could lead to the desired improvement?

3. Just before doing your mental workout, you will take one minute to review your Success Log entries from the

previous day. Looking over your log just before going through your mental work will steer you to emphasize your improvement goals in your mental workout. Hence, the power of goals will be more alive in each and every practice and competition.

Remember, 10-MT takes only about ten minutes per day: four minutes to fill out the Success Log after a practice or game, one minute to review your log before the mental workout, and five minutes for your mental workout. That's ten minutes total. Would you commit ten minutes per day—literally ten minutes—if it meant you would have a proven and concrete way to develop mental toughness and be more mentally prepared for training and competition?

For goals to be kept alive, they need to be consistently used. The 10-MT approach to goal setting works because it helps keep you engaged in practices. Instead of just going through the motions or doing drills to placate coaches, you can become energized about working harder and making improvements.

CHAPTER 7

Personal Rewards Program

Enhancing Motivation

Incentive-laden contracts have become commonplace among professional athletes over the past decade. More and more athletes have "escalator clauses" in their contracts for reaching milestones involving individual statistics, how many games they play, or how many wins the team earns during the season.

Some baseball players tack millions of dollars onto their salaries if they hit a certain number of home runs, win a certain number of games, or record a certain number of saves. Football players often receive workout bonuses for showing up to optional off-season minicamps. Basketball stars often earn bonus money if they are voted to the all-star team during a given season.

Money is definitely a prime motivator for many people, regardless of their profession, but what drives you if you're not being paid to play or compete? In my experience, athletes who establish a "personal rewards" system find it easier and more enjoyable to make the sacrifices necessary to achieve their goals.

A forty-seven-year-old, wealth-management consultant who sought my services for some executive coaching mentioned that he used to be a competitive long-distance runner and had always wanted to run the Boston Marathon, one of the most storied and challenging marathons in the world. Before racing as a qualified runner in the Boston Marathon, entrants must first finish a smaller marathon under a designated time, depending on age and sex. For this client, Rick, that meant running twenty-six miles in less than three and a half hours. For a forty-seven-year-old man who hadn't done any competitive running since college, that was quite a goal. It would require months of concerted distance and strength training.

When it came down to it, Rick was no different from many of the professional athletes who sign contracts with built-in performance incentives. I knew that creating extra incentive for Rick could help with his motivation, just like a major-league pitcher who collects bonus money for every ten innings beyond one hundred that he pitches. I asked Rick to tell me one thing he really wanted to give himself if he qualified for and finished the Boston Marathon. "I really like the look of the Audi A8," he said. "I would love to have that car."

Rick agreed to buy the Audi for himself only after he successfully completed Boston. He ran his first competitive marathon in three hours and twenty-three minutes, qualifying for Boston, where he finished the race in three hours and eighteen minutes. Afterward, Rick cruised to his next session with me in his new Audi A8.

Of course, personal rewards do not have to be material items. During a session with Michelle, a collegiate golfer, I asked, "What have you always wanted to do but haven't yet done?" She told me she had always wanted to go on an African safari to see the elephants, because they fascinated her. At the time of our conversation, Michelle had a twelve-month product goal to make it through Qualifying (Q) School and earn a spot on the LPGA Tour. (Q School for the LPGA Tour consists of two tournaments and three cuts.) I asked Michelle if she would be willing to commit to herself that if and when she made it through Q School, she would reward herself with a trip to Africa to see the elephants. Michelle agreed and pursued her physical and mental preparation.

Although Michelle was diligent in her physical and mental training, she did not make it through the grueling qualifier. A week after missing the cut in the final stage, she joined me for a talk about her future plans. Even though she was upset about not having achieved a paramount goal, she maintained a positive attitude.

"I guess this means I won't be seeing the elephants this year," she told me, "but I will see them soon; I know I can make it through Q School." It took her two more years to battle her way through Q School and join the LPGA Tour, but she never gave up on her dream. For three years, she was relentless in her pursuits, and she finally got to see the elephants.

Rick's story of earning his personal reward was certainly different from Michelle's quest. For both, though, their successes might never have been realized if they had not endowed themselves with that extra incentive to keep plying away.

Goal-Setting Q&A

Each individual must formulate a unique and *effective* goal-setting program. Chapter 6 delineated the three levels of goals (ultimate, product, and process), and in this chapter, you will learn how to set all three levels of goals for yourself. Then, in Chapter 8, you will put all of your new goal information to use to complete your 10-MT Goal Setting for Greatness Work Sheet.

Depending on your skill set, age, and goal, each program will look a little different from all others. The process is simple yet empowering. You'll discover that crafting excellence as a choice rather than a chore eliminates the frustration of training for a goal that seems unreachable. There are four steps you will need to take to personally tailor your 10-MT goal-setting program:

1. Identify what your ultimate accomplishment would be.
2. Determine the specific accomplishments (product goals) necessary to achieve your ultimate goal.
3. For each accomplishment, identify what it will take on your part (process goals) to achieve the goal.
4. Determine the personal sacrifices and character strengths required to live out your dream.

Let's get to it. Take a moment to answer the following questions:

Step 1: Ultimate Goal

What is your ultimate goal in sport?

____

How do you want to be remembered as far as how you prepared and competed?

____

How old do you want to be when you achieve your ultimate goal?

____

Step 2: Product Goals

List two product goals you have for the next competitive season.

____

____

Step 3: Process Goals

For each product goal that you listed, attach two process goals needed to accomplish it. Remember that your process goals are specifically "what it takes" to achieve the product goals.

First product goal: __________________________

Process goal ______________________________

Process goal ______________________________

Second product goal: _________________________

Process goal ______________________________

Process goal ______________________________

Step 4: Strength and Sacrifice

List the two most significant sacrifices it will take to achieve your ultimate goal and next season product goals.

____

____

List your three greatest strengths that confirm that you have what it takes to achieve your ultimate goal and your next season product goals.

____

____

____

Their Goals Versus Your Goals

Sharon, a business client who is an executive in the music industry, once told me, "Goals don't work for me."

"How do you know that?" I asked.

"I never accomplish the goals I set for myself," she replied.

I responded with another question: "What is the last goal you set for yourself?"

"I guess I formally stopped setting goals in high school after I didn't make my goal of getting a college basketball scholarship," she answered.

I asked her to think back to high school. "Do you remember if you took the time to really focus on exactly 'what it takes' to get the attention of college coaches [process goals], or did you mostly focus on getting the college scholarship [product goal]?"

Her answer typified many people's experience with trying to achieve a personal goal: "I really think I was focused on getting the scholarship. I don't remember much other than really putting a lot of pressure on myself during games where I knew college coaches were in the stands. I do remember that my parents really wanted me to get that scholarship. I learned how hard it is to actually accomplish some goals. I guess I just gave up on setting goals. It's not that I don't think goals could help—it's just hard to be motivated to use goals when things don't go your way."

Goals are supposed to add to motivation, and people benefit much from choosing goals that are inherently motivational. The worthiest goals are the ones that produce true happiness. Many times, we are pressured into setting goals to make others happy. You must choose goals that make *you* happy if you want to truly be motivated to achieve them.

The Ins and Outs of Effective Goals

The 10-MT goal-setting program relies on **vision integrity** and **personal incentive style** to help individuals maintain the motivation and commitment necessary for success.

> **Vision integrity:** An attribute of goals aligning a person's hopes and dreams for the future with positive daily decisions.
> **Personal incentive style:** Incentives that are congruent with an individual's personal reward preferences.

Vision integrity differs somewhat from your ultimate goal for any particular sport or competition. It has more to do with your life in general, which includes sports but is not limited to athletics. To figure out your personal vision, you must figure out *who* you want to be and *how* you want to live. In other words, what kind of life do you want for yourself, and what things do you want to accomplish? How do you want to go about becoming that person and fulfilling your aspirations?

Vision integrity is the guidepost for living your life. The "vision" part comes from identifying the three most important aspects of your life that you want to prioritize. For example, Vince Lombardi always said what mattered most was God, family, and the Green Bay Packers. His vision in life was to have a strong relationship with God, be a great husband and father, and achieve excellence in his career as a football coach. The three priorities for Lombardi were God, family, and the Green Bay Packers (career).

The "integrity" portion of vision integrity is living your life on a daily basis in a way that will help you achieve your vision. A person makes thousands of decisions every day. Let your vision be the guide in making those decisions. Have the integrity to live each minute of every day in a manner that will bring you closer and closer to your vision. To have integrity takes a tremendous amount of insight (you must know what your vision is) and discipline. Coach Lombardi is a classic example of an individual who lived his life with vision integrity. Numerous books have been written documenting Lombardi's motivation, commitment, and perseverance to his vision. He was clear on what he wanted and he made decisions each and every day that helped him realize his goals.

Be sure that your ultimate, product, and process goals for sport fall in line with your vision and strive to have integrity everyday. Ask yourself on a daily basis, What are the three most important things in my life? Will my actions today reflect my priorities? Try to make decisions that will help you accomplish your product and ultimate goals for sport, as well as your vision for life, and your success and happiness may grow as large as Coach Lombardi's.

In the foreword to *Mind Gym*, by Gary Mack, Alex Rodriguez wrote about being nine years old in Miami and dreaming of one day becoming a major-league baseball player. He related, "The dream was a little blurry back then and it disappeared when I quit baseball and took up basketball. I wanted to become the next Magic Johnson or the next Larry Bird. Then one day I was talking with my mother and my older brother and I realized that there aren't too many Dominicans playing in the NBA. So after a two-year layoff, I started playing baseball again and that picture in my head, that dream, came back to me. That blurry image started taking focus."[1]

Rodriguez's decision to go back and pursue baseball over basketball is similar to the process many young athletes go through as they are developing vision integrity. It is easy to look back at A-Rod's choice and label it a no-brainer—he may one day hit eight hundred home runs and go down in history as one of the best baseball players ever. However, at that critical plateau in his life, he questioned whether basketball would be more fulfilling. By staying true to his personal vision, he prevented himself from straying too far from the sport he truly loved and in which he was destined to excel for a long time to come.

Defining your personal vision is essential to selecting the right goals. If you do not invest a little time to figure out with some precision who you want to be and how you want to live, you may well select goals to which you will not stay committed. Being the athlete that A-Rod is, it is feasible for him to have become an all-star basketball player had he put the necessary work into it. All that hard work he put into becoming a top hitter could have been spent becoming a top basketball shooter. In the end, his pride as a Dominican and the encouragement of his family led him along the path that he'd envisioned for himself ever since he was in elementary school. It sounds like the logical outcome, but I can testify from personal experience that professional athletes do not always enjoy playing the sport they are paid to play. As a consequence, even success can be bitter. I believe the most important aspect of selecting goals is to make sure the goals you select go along with your personal vision.

The Joy of Vision Integrity

As it turned out, Sharon was not setting goals for herself with vision integrity. She liked basketball and appreciated that she was skilled at the sport, but she didn't "love" it. In fact, she says in retrospect, her parents wanted her to get that basketball scholarship more than she did. Sharon's true interest and passion lay in becoming a musician, but she did not go after this personal vision, yielding instead to external pressure from her parents and teammates to continue playing basketball.

If the motivation behind your selected goals is anything other than true passion and love, then the reward attached to their ultimate accomplishment will be irrelevant. Choose goals for which you have passion, and participate in activities that you enjoy. A good many athletes become strained over time from participating in a sport that always feels like work to play.

I don't mean to imply that sports should always be fun. Sometimes they take serious sacrifice and commitment.

Nevertheless, if you have set goals congruent with who you want to be and how you want to live, it will be much easier for you to muster the self-discipline essential for working through the tough times, and you will be much more likely to achieve great things.

If identifying your aims has you stumped, consider using a methodology for choosing goals that Tal Ben-Shahar endorses. Dr. Ben-Shahar's course on positive psychology has become one of Harvard's most popular courses. In his book *Happier,* he outlines a process of selecting goals that produce happiness: First, make a list of all the activities that you know you are good at. Second, of all the activities you are good at, make note of those activities that you enjoy doing. Then go even further by selecting the activities from that list that you *really* like to do. Once you have that list, go one step further and note the activities that you *really, really* like to do. Those are the activities on which you should focus.

Again, don't confuse what others want with what you want. To verify that you have selected goals with vision integrity, it's necessary create a vision for yourself of who you want to be and how you want to live. Identify the three most important priorities in your life and create a mental image of what your life will look like when you have those in place. Keeping that detailed picture in mind, ask yourself if the ultimate, product, and process goals for sport that you previously listed will in fact bring you closer to your vision. If they will, then it is likely that you'll actually enjoy the hard work necessary for accomplishing those goals.

The integrity part entails your taking the action needed to accomplish your personal vision. You will have to make the decision to commit to your process goals on a daily basis. If you have the vision and the integrity, you will experience a more encompassing sense of enjoyment while you work toward accomplishing your goals, and you will be much more likely to prevail in whatever you do.

Your Own Pursuit of Happiness

A number of years ago, I worked with a young gymnast who was loaded with talent. As a young man, he was ranked as one of the top twenty gymnasts in the country for his age-group. He had already made the Junior National Team and was on the developmental track that many Olympic gymnasts follow. The downside is that he didn't really love gymnastics. The activity that was his passion was diving, even though he wasn't nearly as accomplished a diver as he was a gymnast.

After months of trying to help him rediscover the motivation needed for the intense twenty-four hours of training per week, I realized that his heart wasn't in it. He simply didn't enjoy gymnastics enough. It wasn't fun for him, and it was becoming increasingly difficult to summon the commitment necessary to accomplish his Olympic dream. Finally he decided to give up gymnastics. Initially, he felt strange not going to practice every night, and he eventually started to get into his diving again. He loved going to practice—he once told me that even ordinary diving practices were more fun for him than going to the movies. Upon graduation from high school, he was ranked among the country's top five platform divers, and he had scholarship offers to virtually every collegiate diving program in America.

Whatever a person chooses to do, there will be times when the commitment needed for greatness isn't fun. Working hard is not always enjoyable, but if you love what you do, committing to the hard work will be easier. The reluctant gymnast tried to work through his motivational shortfall for an entire year before he opted to quit gymnastics and focus on diving. As a rule, I believe athletes should not quit any sport prior to the season's end. Try to make things better by talking with the coach before making a decision to leave any sport. If the season ends and you and the coach haven't brought forth anything that helps, reevaluate if leaving the sport is in your best interest.

Human beings are inspired by goals; we experience happiness from striving to achieve them. Research strongly suggests that pushing to reach a goal provides more happiness than actually reaching the goal. It is all about the journey. We need goals in our lives to be happy. Make sure you get yourself involved in an activity that allows and encourages you to set goals for yourself. Life is a precious gift; do the things that pack it with enjoyment for you.

Getting a Grip on Personal Rewards

Here is another method of measuring how much vision integrity your goals have. Think about the sport you emphasized in your lists of goals earlier in this chapter. On a scale of one through ten (where one is very little enjoyment and ten is as much enjoyment as possible), rate how much enjoyment participating in that sport brings you. Don't think about the joy that winning brings; this rating pertains to your participation in general. If your enjoyment level is seven or above, it is probably worthwhile for you to continue striving to be your best in that activity.

The 10-MT personal rewards program allows individuals to identify the specific type of motivation needed

Material reward: A tangible item that is a desirable possession. Examples include a new watch, a clothing item, cash, and even a new car.

Experiential reward: A reward that emphasizes a positive experience. Examples include taking a cruise and spending a day at the spa.

for optimal personal success. Distinguishing between **material rewards** and **experiential rewards** helps determine what combination balance works best. Additionally, it is helpful to be able to call on a supporting mentor, coach, or parent as you strive toward your ultimate goal. Experiential and material rewards are the two types of incentives that enhance people's motivation for goal achievement.

For many of us, taking a $15,000 vacation to Africa or buying an $80,000 car is not financially realistic. That's OK: rewarding ourselves for achieving goals doesn't have to break the bank. The solution is to search for something meaningful that can symbolize your accomplishment. Rewards can be as simple as eating your favorite meal at your favorite restaurant or displaying a trophy or medal that you won.

I know a twenty-four-year-old, Olympic silver medalist who had a photograph blown up, framed, and hung in her house that shows her on the Olympic medal stand during the national anthem. She is reminded of that special moment in her life every time she walks by that picture, and it helped her prepare for competition in the Beijing Olympic Games. Choose an incentive that will bring you pleasure, but do not present yourself that reward until you complete your goal. The incentive should be something that will help you make the sacrifices needed along the way. And be sure to pay up once you achieve your desired goal.

To identify the type of reward that best suites you, complete the following simple questionnaire:

Personal Rewards Program Questionnaire

1. In the past, material rewards have been helpful in keeping me focused and motivated to achieve my goals.

1	2	3	4	5
Strongly disagree	Disagree	Neutral	Agree	Strongly agree

2. In the future, material rewards will be helpful in keeping me focused and motivated to achieve my goals.

1	2	3	4	5
Strongly disagree	Disagree	Neutral	Agree	Strongly agree

3. Material rewards seem to be more helpful than experiential rewards in keeping me focused and motivated to achieve my goals.

1	2	3	4	5
Strongly disagree	Disagree	Neutral	Agree	Strongly agree

4. List one material item that will help motivate you to make the sacrifices necessary to accomplish your goals. (The material item must be financially reasonable.)

____

Material Rewards Score (total from questions 1–3):

____

5. In the past, experiential rewards have been helpful in keeping me focused and motivated to achieve my goals.

1	2	3	4	5
Strongly disagree	Disagree	Neutral	Agree	Strongly agree

6. In the future, experiential rewards will be helpful in keeping me focused and motivated to achieve my goals.

1	2	3	4	5
Strongly disagree	Disagree	Neutral	Agree	Strongly agree

7. Experiential rewards seem to be more helpful than material rewards in keeping me focused and motivated to achieve my goals.

1	2	3	4	5
Strongly disagree	Disagree	Neutral	Agree	Strongly agree

8. List one experiential reward that will help motivate you to make the sacrifices necessary to accomplish your goals. (The reward must be financially reasonable.)

____

Experiential Rewards Score (total from questions 5–7):

____

To determine if you are more motivated by material items or experiential activity, compare your scores from the two sections. If your total from questions 1–3 exceeds your total from questions 5–7, then you are mostly motivated by material rewards, and vice versa. If the two totals are the same or within three points of each other, then you are motivated by both types of rewards.

Whether you go for the material or the experiential, commit to treating yourself with whatever reward you elect (questions 4 and 8) within three months of attaining your goal. Once again: make it something within your means, and withhold it until you've fulfilled your mission. You are also allowed to change your goals and rewards, although people should refrain from doing so repeatedly in a short period. If Michelle had never made the LPGA Tour, for example, she still could have taken her African safari if she had attached the reward to some other important personal goal.

If you will spend the relatively short amount of time required to choose ultimate, product, and process goals with vision integrity, then there should be minimal changing of goals and utmost commitment to them. Still, some shifting and redirecting is normal and appropriate. For young athletes and athletes unsure of what sports they most enjoy, I strongly endorse trying other sports as long as you are not changing in midseason.

If you are reaching every goal, you are not setting your goals high enough. Coming up short on a goal is not a sign of failure. A goal-setting program is of real use only when goal setting helps you accomplish something you would not have otherwise accomplished. Learn to let goals increase your effort to the stage at which you are doing everything in your power to exceed your dreams. Individuals who truly put everything they have into achieving their objectives can be proud of themselves even with goals they don't fully reach. Set goals that will lead to greatness, and you will maximize your athletic potential.

It is also important to set new goals once a goal is achieved. Remember that you stand to experience more joy and satisfaction from striving to reach your goals than from actually achieving them. So, keep replacing achieved goals with bright, shiny new ones.

CHAPTER 8

Tapping the Power of Goals

Train Hard Enough to Make Competition Easy

The value of goals has been widely measured and established beyond doubt. In fact, what two of the most prominent researchers on the subject, Edwin Locke and Gary Latham, discovered after years of research on thousands of people is that the most successful men and women in the world use goals as their primary method of motivation.

College basketball coach Rick Pitino noted that the difference between dreams and goals is that dreams are where we want to end up and goals are how we get there. Essentially what goals do is increase people's motivation. Athletes need motivation to train for hours at high intensity. Goals help people give their best. Vince Lombardi once said, "The harder you work, the harder it is to surrender." I believe it is a realistic expectation to give 100 percent effort 100 percent of the time. What does it mean to give your best? The way to tell if you're giving 100 percent effort is to do everything you know you have to do to be your best.

This doesn't mean you train during every waking hour, day in and day out. For one thing, it is necessary to incorporate rest into training cycles. What it does mean is that if you know of something that would help your training and competitive performance, you owe it to yourself to at least test it out. An example from my practice is a swimmer who thought that improving his flexibility could increase his range of motion enough to eventually lengthen his stroke and thus cut valuable time off his races.

He consulted with a flexibility and posture specialist at the Olympic Training Center, and sure enough, by improving his shoulder flexibility, he was able to trim his race times. It doesn't always play out so neatly. There will be times when you try things that don't do much for you. You have to keep an open mind and channel energy into researching ways to improve. Be willing to do everything that you think could help.

For the 10-Minute Toughness mental-training program to work, there must be effort. I push my clients to train hard enough to make competition easy. I want you to feel confident that you've done everything you know to do to be successful before you start competition. That is what I call preparation. If you are mentally and physically prepared for competition, you stoke your self-confidence. A soccer player with whom I work remarked, "When I step on the field, I know I am more physically and mentally ready than anyone else out there. I work hard, and I know I can play well. I know we are going to win."

Preparing for the Competition

The two keys to being fully prepared and having unwavering confidence in yourself are, first, to put the time and energy into doing everything you know you need to do to be prepared and, second, to be aware that you are fully prepared. You will gain from knowing you have done everything in your power to ready yourself for the event in question, and that confidence will emanate from you throughout. The opposite also pertains: if you have an idea of something that might be helpful for your training but choose not to follow through, when you go into competition, you will know that you haven't done everything in your power to be at your best. This will put you in a weakened position, because you are forfeiting the natural confidence that preparation imparts.

Here is an exercise I like to do with my clients to help quantify how much effort is needed in training to be fully prepared:

1. Write down the name of your toughest competitor, the person you most enjoy outperforming (preferably, not someone on your team).

   ____

2. On a scale of one to ten (where one is very little effort and ten is as much effort as possible), how much effort do you think this person puts into training?

   1 2 3 4 5 6 7 8 9 10

3. On the same scale, how much effort do you put into training?

   1 2 3 4 5 6 7 8 9 10

If you gave yourself a number less than ten, what changes would need to be made for you to feel as though you are putting a ten-level effort into your training? (Avoid citing reasons you can't accomplish a ten; answer only what the ten would look like.)

____

____

I am a firm believer in the precept that winning versus losing is determined more on training days than on game days. I think the person or team who prepares more fully in training wins more often. Let your toughest competitor spur you to become better and better. Every day, pledge to outwork your rivals and put an effort rating of ten into your training. You will guarantee yourself of being more prepared for your opponents than they are for you.

MP100 + 20

You may think you need to train for longer and longer hours to be fully prepared. Sometimes it isn't obvious when enough is enough already. Don't forget that your body needs rest. You can't accomplish the objective of doing everything you know how to do if you overdo it with training. This is where goals come front and center. Let them help you keep structure in your training so that you can feel fully prepared without going to extremes. From a training standpoint, I use the **MP100 + 20** approach for work ethic and training. "MP100" means following 100 percent of your mental-training program and 100 percent of your physical-training regimen, and the "+ 20" symbolizes an additional 20 percent of energy put forth to make sure you are more prepared than the competition.

MP100 + 20: A training approach that requires completing 100 percent of both mental-training and physical-training routines plus 20 percent above and beyond the status quo.

Lanny Bassham, an Olympic gold medal shooter, says that 5 percent of the people do 95 percent of the winning. I concur. Only 5 percent of your competitors will be willing to do everything their coaches tell them plus 20 percent beyond from their own ideas for improvement. You are virtually guaranteed success in life if you consistently perform in the top 5 percent.

If the coach advises you to shoot one hundred free throws, then that is exactly what you do. Ninety-nine free throws will not produce the *true* self-confidence essential for you to perform at your best. It may be subconscious, but something inside of you will know you have not fully delivered on your training plan. Most coaches these days have specific training plans for athletes. Set a goal to follow the training plan 100 percent of the time. For your mental conditioning, do the same: set a goal to follow your mental-training plan 100 percent of the time. If you complete your mental workouts before every practice and game, and you do everything your coach asks of you in practice, you should feel certain that you are fully prepared (MP100).

In addition to adhering to 100 percent of the physical- and mental-training plans, root out a way to personally contribute 20 percent more effort. Find a means to do a little extra from both the physical and mental standpoints. On the physical front, that may translate to spending an extra two hours per week taking ground balls and working on your swing in the cage. Some of the athletes I counsel have such tight schedules that they don't have additional hours at hand, so instead they add 20 percent to every assignment the coach gives them. For example, if the coach wants them to bench-press three sets of ten at a given weight, they might do three sets of twelve. In such cases, you must make sure that the intensity of training stays the same; do not allow more reps to equal less intensity.

An example of +20 on the mental side might be doing the mental workout twice a day at times or committing to using more visualization during competition. It may also be spending more time breaking game film down. Use MP100 + 20 as a guideline. Always look to do a little more than what is expected. If you do 100 percent, you will be only as good as the coach wants you to be; by topping off that effort with + 20, you can be as good as you want to be.

Athletes who subscribe to MP100 + 20 tell me they often feel that their training is harder than competition. When athletes begin to feel as if competition is easier than training, that is an undeniable sign that they are prepared from head to toe and supremely confident.

Your Tool Kit for Success

My goal is to provide you with the best mental-training program for excelling at your sport, and I want it simple and concrete. The 10-MT program asks you to undertake three steps that will take you no more than ten minutes per day in all:

1. Fill out the Goal Setting for Greatness Work Sheet once a year. Place it somewhere you will see it on a regular basis.
2. Perform your mental workout before practices and competitions.
3. Complete your Success Log after every practice and competition; review it just prior to completing your mental workout before the next day's practice or competition.

Filled-in samples, including a form to record your mental workout, appear at the end of this chapter, and blank forms for you to use are provided in Appendix B (remember to copy them first if you'd like to reuse them) and on my website at mysportsworld.com. Completing the work sheets helps athletes with their mental training, as I can attest from personal experience with my clients. In performing this task, you will assemble your personalized tool kit for success. Place your work sheets in a folder, and keep it in a place that is easily accessible before and after practice and competitions. Many of my clients stash their folders in their lockers or gym bags.

You don't need to worry about making your entries letter perfect. The important part of entering the information is undergoing the process from start to finish. There will be days when you will need to fight to get through your mental work, just as practicing or training on certain days feels better than on others. It won't matter if you miss a day or two here and there, and don't be concerned if on some days the work feels better than on others. Your work doesn't need to be pristine, but you do need to get your work done.

Jim Loehr and Tony Schwartz expound on the power of goals and rituals in their groundbreaking book *The Power of Full Engagement.* Rituals are the act of creating positive habits. Rituals occur when individuals connect positive behaviors to specific times, days, and dates. For instance, let's say that instead of going about completing your goal sheet arbitrarily once a year and reviewing it monthly during the season, you commit to completing your goal sheet one month after the season ends and reviewing it on the fifth of every month during the season. How can you make sure this happens? Mark the dates on your calendar. Remember, for goals to work for you, you will have to work for them.

Once you have blocked out your goals and your personal vision, you owe it to yourself to give your best effort to meet those challenges. Giving your best effort means doing anything that will help you become the slightest bit better, and the research clearly confirms the benefit inherent in using goals. The 10-MT goal-setting program relies on seven principles for optimal effectiveness. Here's a recap:

1. **Process over product.** Each day, focus on your process goals, or "what it takes" to achieve your product goals.
2. **No excuses.** Take full accountability for growth by not offering excuses for underachieving.
3. **Go public.** Write your goals down, and tell others what they are, to increase your consciousness of your goals and your accountability for reaching them.
4. **Keep goals alive.** On a daily basis, fill out your Success Log to enhance motivation and results in practices and competitions.
5. **Vision integrity.** Choose goals aligned with who you want to be and how you want to live.

6. **Personal reward preference.** Attach rewards to your goals to burnish motivation and commitment.
7. **MP100 + 20.** Let goals embellish and control your work ethic by aspiring to follow 100 percent of training plans and committing a further 20 percent of your energy into outworking the competition.

When you make it a habit to use Success Logs after each practice or competition, you will be utilizing the seven principles on a regular basis, as the Success Log questions are purposely designed with the principles in mind. Whether the context is sport, business, or even a facet of your personal life, if you will complete the Goal Setting for Greatness sheet yearly and use Success Logs daily, you will enhance your productivity and results.

Always Take Your Best Shot

Training should never become so grueling that it affects your performance in competition. Think of +20 as similar to an on-deck batter swinging a weighted bat before going to the plate. When that hitter gets to the plate with his normally weighted bat, swinging will feel easier, because the practice swings took extra strength. As an athlete, you need to push yourself hard enough in practice so you feel completely prepared in competition.

Mental and physical training is all about putting yourself in the ideal position to succeed. If you are diligent in your preparation, your ability and your confidence will follow closely behind, and you will be able to successfully confront the most imposing challenges.

10-MINUTE TOUGHNESS

Goal Setting for Greatness Work Sheet
Division I Collegiate Quarterback

1. What are the three greatest priorities in your life (please list them in order of importance)?

1. God

2. My family

3. My career in football

Create an image in your mind of what you would like your life to be like ten years in the future, including as much detail as possible related to your three greatest priorities.

Being inducted into the Professional Football Hall of Fame in Canton, Ohio, as the quarterback with the highest completion percentage and most wins. I see myself giving my induction speech, and I can see a number of my teammates there. I see my coaches there, and I also see my parents and my wife there. I am in love with my wife and happy as a good dad to my kids. I see myself as a good man, honest and spiritual and giving back to the community.

2. What is your ultimate goal in sport? (Be sure your ultimate goal has vision integrity.)

My ultimate goal in sport is to become a Hall of Fame NFL quarterback.

3. **List one product goal for the upcoming season and three process goals needed to accomplish it:**

   Product goal: *Lead my team to a conference championship.*

   Process goal: *Be present for and be a team leader at* ***every*** *practice, including weight room (P100).*

   Process goal: *Complete Mental Workouts and Success Logs for every practice and game (M100).*

   Process goal: *Spend at least 30 minutes after practice every day with at least one of the receivers working on 3- and 5-step-drop timing routines (P + 20).*

4. **List a second product goal for the upcoming season and three process goals needed to accomplish it:**

   Product goal: *70 percent completion percentage.*

   Process goal: *Be present for and be a team leader at* ***every*** *practice, including weight room (P100).*

Process goal: *Complete mental workouts and Success Logs for every practice and game (M100).*

Process goal: *Spend at least 30 minutes after practice every day watching game film of upcoming event (M + 20).*

5. **Describe a material or experiential incentive you will use to reward yourself once you accomplish your season product goal.**

   I am motivated by both material and experiential rewards, so I am going to give myself one for each product goal. Conference champs—a really cool piece of abstract art I have been looking at; 70 percent completion percentage—one of three things: hot-air balloon ride, hang gliding, or skydiving.

6. **List the sacrifices it will take on your part for you to achieve your ultimate sport goal.**

   I will miss out on a lot of social stuff, and I will miss a lot of time with my girlfriend as well.

7. **List your character traits that show proof that you have what it takes to achieve your ultimate sport goal.**

   I am a very disciplined and strong person. I know I have the work ethic and talent to accomplish my goals.

8. **Name a coach or mentor who will review your goals progress by the fifth of every month.**

   Jason Selk will review my goals every month.

10-MINUTE TOUGHNESS

The Mental Workout Work Sheet
Division I Collegiate Quarterback

The five parts of my 10-MT mental workout are:

1. *Centering breath*
2. *Performance statement*
3. *Personal highlight reel*
4. *Identity statement*
5. *Centering breath*

The time it takes me to complete my centering breath is:

6-2-7 (15 seconds)

The one most important thought that helps me compete at my best is (this is my performance statement):

Read, set, follow through.

My ideal arousal state is: *6.5*

The three parts of my personal highlight reel (including specific highlights) are:

Part 1: *Past Success Bowl Game, 2006*

- *1st quarter—scramble and big play downfield*
- *2nd quarter—touchdown throw to take the lead*

- *3rd quarter—1st drive of the 2nd half, sharp throws*
- *4th quarter—last drive of the game, making plays to win*
- *Greatest single moment in sport (freeze-frame photo): In the locker room after the game, remembering how great I felt*

Part 2: *Next Elevated-Pressure Competition/Game Conference Championship, 2007 (emphasize "Read, set, follow through" on each throw and 6.5 ideal arousal state)*

- *Strong warm-up—feeling calm and confident and quick; arm feels strong and solid*
- *1st drive of game—mentally sharp, 6.5 ideal arousal state, quick feet, accurate throws (one 3-step drop, one 5-step drop)*
- *2nd drive of game—mentally sharp, 6.5 ideal arousal state, quick feet, accurate throws (one 3-step drop, one 5-step drop)*
- *1st drive of 2nd half—mentally sharp, 6.5 ideal arousal state, quick feet, accurate throws (one 3-step drop, one 5-step drop)*
- *Last drive of game—mentally sharp, 6.5 ideal arousal state, quick feet, accurate throws (one 3-step drop, one 5-step drop)*

Part 3: *Next Competition/Game First Game of the Season, 2007 (emphasize "Read, set, follow through" and 6.5 ideal arousal state on each throw)*

- *Strong warm-up—feeling calm and confident and quick; arm feels strong and solid*
- *1st drive of game—mentally sharp, 6.5 ideal arousal state, quick feet, accurate throws (one 3-step drop, one 5-step drop)*
- *2nd drive of game—mentally sharp, 6.5 ideal arousal state, quick feet, accurate throws (one 3-step drop, one 5-step drop)*
- *1st drive of 2nd half—mentally sharp, 6.5 ideal arousal state, quick feet, accurate throws (one 3-step drop, one 5-step drop)*
- *Last drive of game—mentally sharp, 6.5 ideal arousal state, quick feet, accurate throws (one 3-step drop, one 5-step drop)*

The self-image statement that reminds me that I have what it takes to be a great athlete is (this is my identity statement):

I have the talent and the drive; I am the most accurate passer in the country.

The best times for me to complete my mental workout (centering breath—performance statement—personal highlight reel—identity statement—centering breath) are:

I will complete my mental workouts about 20 minutes before every practice and game and in the evenings as I go to sleep (when needed).

10-MINUTE TOUGHNESS

Success Log
Division I Collegiate Quarterback

"I've always believed that if you put in the work, the results will come. I don't do things half-heartedly. Because I know if I do, then I can expect half-hearted results."

—Michael Jordan

1. What three things did I do well today?

- *Completed my mental workout and Success Log.*
- *Stayed after practice for seventy-five minutes (timing routes and game film).*
- *Stayed on top of my studies.*

2. Based on today's performance, what do I want to improve?

My accuracy on throws over 30 yards.

3. What is one thing I can do differently that could lead to the desired improvement?

Spend 10 minutes on long routes every day after practice and plug one long-route completion into the 2nd and 3rd parts of the personal highlight reel.

This Success Log was completed after one of the practices about a third of the way through the season (senior year).

PHASE 3

RELENTLESS SOLUTION FOCUS

CHAPTER 9

Always Have a Solution on the Board

Sports are filled with intriguing stories of underdogs beating the odds. Superior talent can often be deceptive when it is opposed by willpower and a relentless work ethic. In 1980, a bunch of fresh-faced college kids on the United States Olympic hockey team improbably defeated a Soviet Union team that had won five of the previous six gold medals. In 1969, a supposedly inferior AFL team called the New York Jets won the Super Bowl over the NFL's Baltimore Colts in a game that forever changed the perception of the two leagues' talent gap.

More recently, in Super Bowl XLII, the New York Giants were two-touchdown underdogs to the previously unbeaten New England Patriots and wound up winning on a last-minute touchdown drive that won't soon be forgotten. Back in 1990, Buster Douglas beat 42-to-1 odds by defeating a peaking Mike Tyson in a boxing match that wasn't supposed to get past the second round. In 2007, Appalachian State stunned a highly ranked Michigan football team playing at home in a game that was supposed to be a de facto early-season "warm-up" for the storied Wolverines. And the list goes on (with your geographical location likely to dictate which notable upsets you remember most).

In all of these instances, a team or athlete shocked the sporting world by pulling off what was seemingly impossible. The chances of these underdogs winning were rated by outsiders as next to zero: showing up and competing was essentially a formality. What these winning teams and players consciously or unconsciously understood was that success isn't built on worrying about all the problems a supposedly superior opponent presents. Excellence is achieved through a solution-focused mind. Simply put, teams like the 1980 U.S. Olympic hockey team and the 2007 New York Giants keep their eyes on what they need to do rather than worrying about how they stack up next to a more "accomplished" opponent. They allow nothing to waylay them, regardless of any statistical evidence that they have precious little chance of winning.

We humans are better at seeing problems than we are at seeing solutions. This itself is a problem, because what we dwell on expands. When we spend most of our lives thinking about problems, we heft an unnecessary weight onto our shoulders. Fortunately, we have the capacity for change. We are able to overcome our human tendency to continuously ruminate on problems and actually become solution focused.

Solution-Focused Sailing

The following fictitious story helps illustrate the difference between a *problem-focused* mind-set and a *solution-focused* mind-set.

A yacht, sailing far offshore in the Atlantic Ocean, was taking on water and sinking, forcing the passengers onto the vessel's two safety boats. For the harried people aboard the safety boats, the outlook was bleak. They could not spy land in any direction, and no one on either boat knew which way to begin paddling. They were undersupplied, cold, and wet, having only the clothes they wore and a few oars. As the boats began to drift apart, the passengers of each boat shared their thoughts as to the best course of action.

One of the safety boats held solution-focused passengers. They decided, based on the location of the sun and their best guess of their starting point, to face the boat due west and begin paddling in shifts so that they could all take turns working and resting.

The second boat, which carried problem-focused passengers, came to a different conclusion. Each time someone suggested a possible solution, someone else argued against the plan, finding reasons for its assured failure. The problem-focused crew members became convinced that rowing to land was impossible, as they were at least three hundred miles from the nearest shoreline; they had no food or water; the safety boats were not built to withstand the ripping winds and stormy seas of the Atlantic; and they were all soaked to the bone, shivering, and exhausted. Eventually, they deemed their situation hopeless. They attempted to convey their fears and despair to the companion safety boat, but to no avail, as it was already too far away for its passengers to hear their wails.

The solution-focused boat paddled on, with everyone working in shifts and fixed on survival. Soon, just as the problem-focused brethren had predicted, the solution-focused boat encountered a pronounced northerly wind, making it difficult to proceed at all in the westward direction. Refusing to surrender in the face of the new challenge, they worked to cobble a solution. By fashioning makeshift sails from their shirts, and then sharing the remaining clothing for maximum warmth, the passengers of the solution-focused boat were able to harness the wind and pick up a little speed on their journey toward land.

As these passengers were celebrating their slight but noticeable progress, the problem-focused boat was still in the presence of the sinking yacht, with its hapless passengers clinging to increasingly slim hopes of rescue with rapidly diminishing spirits. Just then, a storm moved in, and both boats began to fill with water. The solution-focused passengers were alarmed, but it never occurred to them to give up. They disassembled their makeshift sails and tied their shirts together to form a rudimentary tarpaulin to keep as much water from accumulating in the boat as possible, while simultaneously using their shoes and caps to bail out the boat. Their boat still took on a lot of water, but through vigorous effort and determination, they were able to keep afloat long enough for the storm to subside. One crew member noted that the falling rain just might save their lives. Although the rain was cold, they were all suffering from dehydration and probably wouldn't make it much longer without drinking water. They began using their shoes not only to bail out the boat but also to capture rainwater for drinking and store it for the future.

Meanwhile, the storm only served to pulverize any hopes among the passengers of the other boat, who had neither the mental discipline nor the spirit to troubleshoot ways to combat the rain or their dehydration. Having made no progress toward land and with their boat rapidly filling with water, the passengers accepted their dismal fate.

After what seemed an eternity, the storm receded, the sun broke through the clouds, and the ocean calmed. The few remaining survivors on the problem-focused boat were grateful for the break in weather, but they knew it was just a matter of time until they too would perish. During this same period, the solution-focused crew members celebrated their victory over the storm and began to feel a renewed determination to survive. They experienced a sense of pride, relief, and satisfaction at the distance they had come, and some even jokingly compared their safety boat to a vacation cruise ship. Knowing that they had beaten the odds, they gained even more confidence in their ability to solve problems together and make it to land alive.

At this point, you obviously see the difference that being solution focused can make. We have likely all been in situations in which we were surrounded by people who focus on the magnitude of problems rather than the merits of solutions. Just the same, at times, all of us have, through frustration or anxiety, been problem focused ourselves. Does the solution-focused boat survive and make it to land? No one can say for sure. However, it stands a much better chance than the problem-focused boat. Which boat do you think teams such as the 1980 U.S. Olympic hockey squad or the 2007 New York Giants would have occupied?

In addition, consider the respective life experiences for the passengers of the two safety vessels. Imagine the experience of hunching in a cold and wet safety boat, feeling helpless in the grips of hypothermia and dehydration. Compare that with the experience of the solution-focused passengers: they did what they could, refused to yield, and endured heartache and trouble, but they also managed to work through catastrophe, and because they were in a solution state of mind, they were open to discovering new ways to use their circumstances to their advantage.

Whether they made it or not, they had the personal satisfaction that they never gave up. They may even have gained experience and knowledge from the ordeal that would allow them to more fully enjoy the rest of their lives, no matter how long or short. In the end, they did what they could, and they kept themselves energized and upbeat with a solution focus. They may well have overcome insurmountable odds and saved their own lives and limbs.

Overcoming Obstacles

The big question for any athlete is this: Which boat are you in? Do you focus on problems or solutions? When adversity bars your way, do you choose to fight to overcome the challenge, or do you let problems intimidate you into slumping to the floor and accepting ready defeat? Do you devise a way to keep going? Do you manufacture a means to uproot all obstacles that impede the path of growth, improvement, and success?

I recently had a client ask me, "What does it really mean to be solution focused?" Being solution focused means keeping your thoughts centered on what you want from life and what it takes to achieve what you want, as opposed to allowing thoughts of self-doubt and concern to occupy the mind. The difference between a solution focus and a *relentless* solution focus is how often you commit to replacing negative thinking with solutions.

Personal research tells me that most people achieve solution-focused thought about 40 percent of the time, while individuals with a *relentless* solution focus replace 100 percent of undesirable thinking with thoughts emphasizing solutions. A hockey coach I know put it to me this way, "Every time I catch myself feeling angry or scared or depressed it is because I am thinking about what I don't have in my life or about something that is wrong with me. The instant I catch myself feeling uncomfortable I ask, 'What is one thing I can do right now that could make my situation better?,' and literally 100 percent of the time things improve. I have trained myself to be relentless. Sometimes I have to ask myself that question fifteen or twenty times over the course of an hour. Whatever it takes, I will keep asking until the shift occurs."

On Friday, October 13, 1972, the most unbelievable real-life example of having a relentless solution focus began to unfold. At 8:00 A.M., the Old Christians rugby team left the Uruguayan Air Force Base on a twin turboprop airplane headed for a match in Santiago, Chile. The team would never make it to the match. At 3:30 that afternoon, as players tossed the rugby ball around the cabin, the aircraft crashed into the Andes Mountains. On the morning of October 14, twenty-seven of the original forty-five passengers were miraculously alive and waiting to be rescued on the mountain.

When three days on the mountain had come and gone, they realized that help was not on the horizon and set about preparing to rescue themselves. Combing the wreckage, they built a rudimentary hospital-shelter out of the fuselage to help them brave the frigid temperatures and constructed a water-making device so that they'd have sterile water to drink and use to clean wounds. With no food available, they were forced to eat the flesh and organs of those who had perished.

To compound their horror, after their seventeenth day on the mountain, an avalanche hit, enclosing them in a certain snow tomb. Still, the survivors refused to give up. They huddled together for warmth and fought for their lives over the next three days, until nineteen of them clawed their way out. On day sixty-two of their battle for survival on the mountain, two teammates decided to try to hike to civilization. They climbed for ten days in below-zero temperatures across some of the steepest and most unrelenting mountains in the world, and eventually Nando Parrado and Roberto Canessa made it to safety. Remaining solution focused and pushing themselves to the limits of human endurance for seventy-two days eventually saved sixteen of the original survivors.

As certain death hovered ever closer, sixteen individuals rejected failure and survived the impossible. Early on, they set a clear goal for themselves: do whatever is necessary to stay alive. They stayed focused on what it would take to survive and, no matter what the circumstance, found a way to accomplish their goal.

Although staying solution focused isn't usually a life-or-death proposition, it is essential in a person's quest for success. Numerous self-help books, including Norman Vincent Peale's *The Power of Positive Thinking* and the ever-popular *The Secret,* have talked conceptually about the need to keep your mind focused on the prize. The 10-MT model—always have a solution on the board—goes beyond concept to provide you with a simple and concrete tool that has been proven to help individuals develop and maintain a solution-focused approach to sport and life.

Keep Your Eye on the Prize

Consider the following diagram:

Problems	Solutions

Let's assume the chart represents the chalkboard of your life. On which side of the board have you spent the most time making entries? If you are like most people, you have spent most of your time operating from the "Problems" side. The human mind, as we know, is biologically predisposed to be more sensitive to problems, and because of this, we are likely to be problem focused. Whenever people get together, a logical topic of discussion is problems. We all have problems. It is natural to focus on problems, and that is what we talk about with each other.

All this thinking and talking about problems only nurtures the existence of more problems. Let me give you another slant on this concept: The most valuable resource for human beings is oxygen; without oxygen, we die within minutes. However, the last time you realized just how wonderful it is to have air to breathe is probably the last time you were deprived of it. Furthermore, when you watch or read the news, what are the stories usually about—problems or solutions? When you watch a TV drama or a film, how much time is devoted to the problem, compared with the time spent on the solution?

The fact is that we are better at seeing problems than we are at seeing solutions, and this phenomenon creates more problems. It's a vicious cycle that many of us get trapped in; by being problem focused, we end up doubling our losses. There is little doubt that if we spend most of our lives on the "Problems" side of the board, we can expect our time on Earth to be marked by perpetual worry. We need not despair, though, because we have the capacity for change. With the right tools we can overcome our human imperative to focus on problems and instead become solution focused.

Pursuing Excellence

My job as a sport psychology consultant is to help people maximize their potential, set high goals, and remove roadblocks that thwart success. I set out, in my work, to locate the key that unlocks people's hidden potential to prevail against obstacles and emerge victorious. When athletes are short on their supply of confidence, I remind them to "always have a solution on the board."

In sports (and in life), there is always potential for growth. Even Tiger Woods spent time revamping his swing to improve his game in the midst of an already enormously successful career. There are always things you can do better if you pore over solutions to weaknesses. An Olympic gold medal wrestling coach once told me that there are two principal types of athletes, those with talent and those with work ethic, and the greatest athletes possess both. Underdogs such as the 1980 U.S. Olympic hockey team exemplify the maxim that while you may not be able to control talent, you can always control work ethic.

Making the commitment to acquire and retain a solution focus will complement your mental workouts and goal setting. The solution-focused mind-set will spur you to continually upgrade your 10-MT mental-training plan. A case in point from my practice is a collegiate basketball player. This young man is a cocaptain on the team and its leading scorer. His team had just won its first game in the NCAA tournament, yet he didn't play as well as he would have liked. After the game, he was dejected and upset with himself and his play.

He told me that he was disappointed in his aggressiveness on offense. He said that he was driving only when there was an open lane, and he knew that as the competition got tougher, it would become harder to create offense. He also knew that if he forced himself to drive more even when the defense was tight, his team would stand a much better chance of progressing in the tournament. Rather than allow himself to continue to rue his nonaggressive play, he decided to focus on a solution. He knew he needed to create more offense for his team by attacking the defense.

He decided to change his personal highlight reel to better reflect the physical and aggressive offensive "attacking style" he knew he needed. In accordance, he adjusted his identity statement from "I am physical and strong; I am the best scorer in the conference" to "I am physical and strong; I drive every time I touch the ball on offense; I am the best scorer in the tournament." Although his team got beaten in the Sweet Sixteen round, this young man came out ahead by knowing that he had played well. Instead of staying down on himself after registering poor play in the first game of the tournament, he marshalled his solution-focused attitude to search for ways to improve. In the act, he led his team in scoring and assists for the next two games.

CHAPTER 10

The Solution-Focused Tool

When we think about problems, our problems grow. When we think about solutions, our solutions grow. Thinking about solutions makes life much more enjoyable and allows us to become much more successful.

The fly in the ointment is that we are battling human nature when we try to maintain a solution focus over a problem focus. I try to help athletes get their focus where it needs to be—pointed toward success. I ask them to answer the question, "What is one thing I can do that could make this better?" Every time they catch themselves locking onto a problem, I tell them to ask that question and to keep asking until they get a solution that stays "on the board." The solution does not need to produce perfection. It merely has to promote improvement.

You can put small and large problems alike to rest by using a simple, concrete, and highly effective method of changing problem-focused thinking into solution-focused thought. Answering this question sets the mind on the right track toward solving a problem. The solution-focused tool also provides an immediate sense of empowerment, because it allows people to control their own destinies.

The Difference Between Good and Great

About the time I discovered the "What is one thing I can do . . ." tool, I was working with a minor-league pitcher in the Chicago White Sox organization who was young, talented, and hardworking. He didn't have overpowering stuff, but he was eager to learn, and he had an understanding of how to pitch. He and I had many discussions about becoming and staying solution focused.

As he started working his way up through the White Sox farm system, he experienced inconsistencies with his success. He'd have a fine game in which he pitched great, followed by one in which he didn't do so well. Between starts, he would lapse into thinking about what he was doing wrong and pressuring himself to pitch better. His problem-focused rut undermined his ability to consistently pitch the way he wanted and needed to pitch.

I asked him one time how he thought his problem-centric thinking impacted his ability to perform well. "It has a terrible impact," he responded. "The four days in between starts, I can't get this stuff out of my head. It feels like all I do is think about what is wrong and how I am never going to make it at this rate. By the time I get to the field, my confidence is shot. Even though I am doing my mental workouts, I know in the back of my head that there is a problem. If anything starts going wrong, the self-doubt creeps in and takes over. I think it's the reason I haven't made it yet. I know I am smart, talented, and hardworking. I am good enough to pitch in the majors if I could just get out of my own way."

I then asked him how often he was thinking about problems. He said that over the course of a day when he wasn't pitching, he would have anywhere between thirty and one hundred thoughts of self-doubt or problems, and about 60 percent of the time, he would replace the self-doubt with solution-focused thoughts. On pitching days, he said, he would have about the same number of self-doubting thoughts, but he would replace those thoughts with positive visualization or positive self-talk about 90 percent of the time.

I asked him if he could commit to replacing all problem-focused thinking with solution-focused thoughts of how he wanted the next start to go. Specifically, I asked him to replace all negative thinking with either his performance statement, his identity statement, or some positive visualization of how he wanted to pitch in his next start. In essence, I asked him to undergo an abbreviated mental workout. First, he needed to convince himself that his negative thoughts were not helping—research confirms that negative thinking makes it harder to be successful. Next, he needed to commit himself to stop the negative thinking by replacing his problem-focused thoughts with a positive image or statement (similar to the thought replacement discussed in Chapter 4).

Thinking about how poorly he performed against a certain team was hampering this young man's development into the pitcher he knew he could be. While being solution focused 60 percent of the time on nongame days and 90 percent of the time on game days was an improvement for him, it was not enough. I needed to remind him of the difference between a *relentless* solution focus and a solution focus, which is the ultimate measurement of mental toughness. Then I asked him, "What is one thing you can do differently that could help you be solution focused more often?"

He replied, "I think I should focus on nongame days. Really, the big issue is that when I feel anxious about pitching, I try *not* to think about it rather than trying to get the right thoughts into my head. I like the idea of facing my fears head on. If I start feeling nervous about my career, I am going to figure out exactly what it is that I am nervous about and then attach a solution to the problem. I know I can and need to do a better job of that."

On his next outing, he managed to pitch seven strong innings, giving up three hits and one earned run. He was floored by how much of an improvement it made for him to replace his negative thinking on nonpitching days. For the next two years, he dedicated himself to controlling his thoughts and staying intent on how he wanted to pitch.

There were ugly days, and he had some games in which he got knocked around a bit, but he told himself to maintain a solution-focused approach. His consistency remarkably improved, and he is currently a successful pitcher in the big leagues. I no longer work with him, but he recently sent me an e-mail saying thanks and adding that the key to his success is his relentless solution focus. He went on to say that for the last year, he was able to "chase" 100 percent of his negative thoughts by replacing them with thinking centered on how he wanted his next start to go. It was no coincidence that he ended up carving a full run off his career ERA once he began seeking solutions rather than lamenting his problems.

Injury and the Solution Focus

Of course, the medicine (your positive thought) must fit the ailment (the negative thought hampering your performance). Negative thoughts are capable of entering your mind hundreds, if not thousands, of times a day. Ideally, you would be able to counter these thoughts by doing the full 10-MT workout, but obviously you need to have a quicker fix. Pinpoint the one component in your workout—whether it is a specific sequence in your personal highlight reel or your identity statement—that will make it feasible for you to quash every negative thought right away. For the minor-league pitcher, an extract from his personal highlight reel of him performing well against his "problem" team refocused his mind to where he wanted it to be. For other people, the thought-replacement technique may emphasize performance or identity statements.

Another example applies here. I work with one of the top amateur tennis players in the country. In March 2007, at the age of seventeen, she blew out her knee (torn anterior and medial cruciate ligaments) in a tournament. She was in a lot of pain and was naturally discouraged about the injury. She faced a complicated surgery and twelve months of recovery. She easily could have grown despondent and used the injury as an excuse to be lazy and forget about tennis for a while.

Instead, she adopted a solution-focused approach. She set out to find at least one thing she could do while injured that would make her a better player than she was before the injury. Anytime she caught herself feeling sorry for herself, she replaced the mental weakness with convictions about how she would come back stronger because of the injury. She used her injury to motivate action so that once she was healthy again, she could actually look at the injury as a positive experience. She decided to improve her serving strategy and execution. Although she could not stand erect or physically practice her serve, she got down to business studying videos of some of the best tennis players. She put endless hours into identifying what the masterful servers were doing to be masterful.

She looked for specific serves and serving patterns that packed the most wallop and then went about creating her own specifically tailored serving strategy. She overcame numerous obstacles along the way. On days when she was in too much pain to move around, she worked from bed. Coaches were reluctant to meet with her to help her identify patterns, so she bribed them by suggesting that they meet for lunch or by taking them out to dinner. The competitor in her refused to accept any excuse for not turning her injury into an asset. No matter how bad things got, she committed herself to keeping her sights and her mind glued on how she wanted things to be.

She later said that her injury proved more to herself than did any of her on-the-court successes. She said she learned that she was truly a competitor to be reckoned with because of the way she battled through a major trauma. Not only did she come back from injury with a much improved serve, but also she was physically stronger and in better shape than she had ever been in her life. "A lot of people talk about finding the good in bad situations, but I really did it," she relayed. "I proved to myself that

I truly can do anything when I set my mind to it. Now nothing really gets to me. I have learned that whatever life throws at me, I can and will get through."

The +1 Concept

People have a tendency to become so overwhelmed with life and all of the things that need to be done that it becomes increasingly difficult to accomplish anything at all. I call this being "overcome by the mountain." Imagine standing at the base of Pikes Peak, with the task of climbing to the summit and back down. You might squint up at the mountain and muse, "Wow, look at how high that mountain is. I can't believe how much work it will take to get to the top." You may even peer around and ask, "Can you believe how long it will take me to get all the way up there?" All the while, you aren't doing the one thing that will get you to the top: putting one foot in front of the other.

Put the **+1 concept** into action to prevent feelings that plague your mind with unnecessary stress. The best way to climb a mountain is to take one step at a time. Coaches and athletes have repeated this "take it one game at a time" platitude ad nauseam in recent years. That's probably because it is such an effective way to make tangible progress without becoming drained emotionally.

+1 concept: The idea that success can be achieved by meeting a string of basic, incremental goals in the present that will ultimately lead to excellence in the future.

For a fitting example of a team using the +1 concept, take the 2004 Boston Red Sox. Down three games to none to the rival New York Yankees in the 2004 ALCS, the Sox refused to give in. They decided to focus on one game at a time, and eventually they climbed back to a decisive seventh game, in which they easily defeated the Yankees, and they went on to play in the World Series. In conformity with the +1 concept, the Red Sox stayed afloat until they gained enough momentum and confidence to become world champions.

Use the +1 concept to begin chipping away at your problems and even the biggest issues will become manageable before long. Individuals oftentimes wait for that perfect pitch before they swing the bat. Or they wait for that perfectly open look at the basket before they shoot. Any good hitter will tell you that you can't hit the ball if you don't swing and any good shooter will tell you that you won't be racking up points without shooting the basketball. Believe in yourself and your ability to make gradual improvements, and the results will follow.

Gradual improvement over time brings about vibrant and sustainable growth. I have observed that when individuals emphasize improvement over perfection, their progress accelerates. We frequently get confounded by how much work it will take for our problems to be completely resolved. We become paralyzed, unable to take action toward improvement. You do not need to arrive at perfection; you need to slowly but surely make things better.

The 1998 NFL season was a trying one for the St. Louis Rams. They finished twenty-fourth out of thirty teams on offense; defensively, only four clubs ranked lower. Their dismal 4–12 record had them tied for last place in their division. For their head coach, Dick Vermeil, it was a tall order to stay solution focused in the presence of so much adversity, but he and his staff went to work in the off-season with a mandate of effecting gradual but consistent improvement.

Offensively, the Rams drafted future–Pro Bowl wide receiver Tory Holt and acquired superstar running back Marshall Faulk from the Indianapolis Colts. Under defensive coordinator Peter Giunta, the Rams also made a commitment to improve the defense. One of the defensive players with whom I worked at the time told me, "The attitude on the defense changed. It was no longer acceptable to be mediocre. Each week, we got a little better. Our confidence grew as a team, and we really started to believe we could be Super Bowl champions."

Going into training camp the next year, the Rams had high spirits. Coaches and players had worked hard, and they knew they were poised to be more respectable and competitive on Sundays. Then the unthinkable happened: their starting quarterback, Trent Green, went down with a season-ending knee injury. Coach Vermeil was forced to start the season with his third-string quarterback, who only twelve months earlier had been stocking shelves in a grocery store. The team could have decided to throw in the towel on the season. Instead, the coaching staff and players, including their new quarterback, Kurt Warner, remained committed to improvement.

The 1999 Rams surpassed all expectations that others held for them. They became known as the "greatest show on turf" thanks to the highest-powered offense in the NFL, and their defense ended the season ranked fourth overall. The Rams went on to beat the Tennessee Titans by 23–16 in one of the most exciting Super Bowls in recent history. The coaching staff's solution-focused persistence cashed in dividends for a team that just a year before was at a franchise low point.

Stories reminiscent of the 1999 Rams pop up in sports all the time. Teams get better as they connect individual pieces of the puzzle. For a football roster with fifty-three players, the +1 concept begins by identifying the right players for a given system. But once the individual players are in the system, how do they improve their individual games to get to that next level?

Emphasizing the +1 concept helps people get started. An old riddle asks, "What is the best way to eat an elephant?" Answer: "One bite at a time." Lanny Bassham, the Olympic gold medal shooter mentioned in Chapter 8, calls this handy precept the "ready, fire, aim" principle. Lanny claims that in sports and in life, people spend too much time aiming at the bull's-eye and not enough time shooting at it. Rather than placing so much emphasis on getting ready and aiming, go ahead and take a shot. Taking the shot gets you started and also lets you gauge how far off the mark you are. Make adjustments, but keep shooting until you get closer and closer, and eventually you will hit the bull's-eye.

The Can't Say "I Don't Know" Game

Can't say "I don't know" game: A solution-based tool that forces participants to get in a problem-solving mode by prohibiting them from giving "I don't know" as an answer.

What inevitably will happen when you begin to use the +1 tool in the face of a problem is that you will ask yourself the operative question—"What is one thing I can do that could make this better?"—and your hair-trigger answer will be, "I don't know." Of course you don't know. If you *did* know, you would have already tried it. When this occurs, I want you to play the **can't say "I don't know" game** with yourself. The first step to figuring out the "I don't know" is to stop saying "I don't know."

Remind yourself that your body listens to what your brain tells it. If you tell yourself you don't know, you're right; by the same token, if you start telling yourself there is a solution, you will also be correct. From now on, when you ask the question, you must come up with an answer. Act as though your life depends on your contributing some form of answer. It doesn't necessarily have to be the right one, but you have to get going on the process, and nothing clogs the process more than the "I don't know" excuse.

I'd like to share an example from my personal life. In January of 2000, my grandmother passed away. She was one of those special people who was always fun to be around. She approached life with a smile, and her attitude was infectious. My grandmother was my best friend up until the time I met my wife, Mara. After that, my grandmother ran a close second. When she died, I missed her terribly. I missed seeing her on holidays, and I missed our weekly two-dollar football, basketball, and baseball bets. I tried and tried to get over her passing and didn't seem to be making headway.

Driving to work one morning, I started to get emotional thinking about how much I missed her. As I drove, I asked myself, "What is one thing I can do that could make this better?" In response, I kept telling myself, "I don't know." Again, I was correct: I didn't know, and I wouldn't ever know if I kept telling myself that I didn't know. So, I played the game. I repeated the query, and then instead of saying I didn't know, I forced myself to think, to analyze my thoughts and sincerely look for a solution. I reminded myself that a solution existed for my problem. I gazed out the car window and imagined that the solution was somewhere out there; I just needed to search until I found it. Then my mind shifted gears, and I thought of something that could possibly help.

I decided to have a party in my grandmother's honor on New Year's Day, her favorite day of the year, and I would call it Genevieve's Day. We would have wonderful food and a slew of guests and even some friendly two-dollar wagering on football. I immediately started to feel better. I got to work on the party and decided to deliver a toast in honor of the special day. The party was a blast, the toast wasn't bad, and we decided to make it an annual event. I would write a new toast every year to honor my grandmother's spirit, her life, and her impact on the people who knew her. What mattered most was that it helped me adjust to my grandmother's death in a more positive, healthy manner. As a result, my life was better because I played the can't say "I don't know" game.

Then there was the baseball player with whom I was working who got drafted by the Anaheim Angels organization. His inaugural year with the Angels' system was not spectacular. For the first time in his life, he had a batting average less than .300. It wasn't necessarily his low batting average that bothered him, though. More so, it was the fact that he was doing everything he knew to do to be successful and was still not hitting with consistency. He felt uncomfortable in the batter's box, and by his own admission, he was underachieving. He tried valiantly to get his swing back: he sought out a variety of coaches and players within the organization to help; he took extra batting practice and spent time alone in the cage searching for his once powerful and trusty swing. Nothing turned the trick.

In one of our phone sessions, I asked him what else he thought he could do. For someone as well versed as he was in the rules of the can't say "I don't know" game, his frustrated response said it all. "I honestly don't know if there is anything else I can do," he told me.

Then something amazing happened. I heard him drop the phone momentarily before blurting that he would call me right back. Ten minutes later, he called again. He said I would not believe what he was about to tell me. He had dropped the phone while we were talking because he had just inadvertently stepped on his eyeglasses and snapped the frame.

He went to his medicine cabinet to get his contact lenses, still pondering what he could do to try to get his swing back. As he pulled out his contacts, he remembered that a year ago, he had gone to the eye doctor just before being removed from his parents' health insurance plan. The eye doctor had noticed that one of his prescriptions was off and was going to send him some new contacts. Right at the time all that was happening, he was drafted by Anaheim, and with all the excitement, he had forgotten to start using the new contacts.

He said, "I just now remembered, my doctor told me it would probably help me see the ball better. I can't believe I forgot." From that day forward, he started using the new contacts, and—miracle of miracles—it was much easier to see the ball. After all his extra work, it wasn't his swing that was out of whack. He eventually rooted out the cure because he continued to search for one. Keeping your mind receptive to solutions—even if they lie in the hands of fate—will allow you to spot promising answers where you didn't even know you needed to look. You may also discover along the way, as this player did, that your skills will improve as a by-product of your pursuit. For this "contact" hitter, all that extra batting practice and discussion about mechanics with his coaches transferred directly to his development as a hitter.

Do All Problems Have Solutions?

You will not stumble across some revelatory solution to every problem, but stories like that of the Angels player led me to another question: Does every problem have a solution? In Dale Carnegie's bestselling book *How to Win Friends and Influence People,* the author hails Abe Lincoln's belief that solutions exist for every problem as one of the former president's chief attributes. Believing in solutions is a vital agent for success, and it started to become clear to me that, indeed, every problem has a solution. It didn't stop there: I started to believe that every problem had numerous solutions. Not every problem has the perfect solution, but all problems can be improved.

If every problem has a solution, does everyone have the personal ability to seize on a means to make things better? This question poses more of a puzzle. My experience is that once people realize that there are solutions out there for every problem, they will become better and better at unearthing them. If you believe that solutions await, you are more likely to persist in your exploration. The more practice you get, the better you will become at discerning them. Finding solutions may not always be smooth sailing, but without a doubt, the undertaking is feasible for you along with everyone else. The key is to know that solutions exist and to search and find them.

Problem Awareness Triggers Problem Solution

At times, individuals begin to feel as if they are their problems. We are not our problems, because we have the ability to recognize that we have problems. This awareness proves that we are separate from—and more powerful than—whatever vexes us. On any given day, something can go wrong, and a person can become so wrapped up in the experience that awareness of anything else is blurred. People say to me all the time, "I didn't stop to think about solutions or problems. All I knew is that I was unhappy [or "mad" or "stressed out"]." This scenario raises another fundamental concept: anytime a person feels uncomfortable, it is a direct response to the perception of a problem. Use this natural alarm system to jump-start the solution-focus process.

Anytime you feel angry, sad, stressed, frustrated, or just generally uncomfortable, seek out and define the underlying problem. Keep it simple, spending as little time and energy as necessary on this step. Once you nail down what is causing you to feel uncomfortable, immediately make the shift to the solution side of the board by asking yourself what one thing you could do differently that could make things better. Use the tool anytime you are uncomfortable or unhappy with life, and keep using it until you get a solution that stays on the board.

Bring Your Solutions to Life

An essential part of the process is to follow through with the solution. People tend to get roadblocked at the juncture of getting a solution on the board. If you do not put action into the solution, your problem is bound to linger. Solutions have only as much energy as you put into them. For example, until that pitcher for the White Sox cited at the beginning of this chapter set about replacing his negative thoughts with tools from his 10-MT workout, his problem festered.

Getting his arms around what he needed to do was only a partial measure. What will eventually transpire without follow-through is that solutions will rub off as you are trying to arrange them on the board. You will come to discredit all of your prospective solutions, because you will know you won't bring them to life. If this is the case, you will post a new problem on the board: *inaction*. You must breathe life into every solution you flag, or keep crossing them out until you get one up that you are willing to charge with energy.

An exercise that I use in my workshops richly illustrates the value of taking action. I stand in front of the audience holding a crisp, new one-hundred-dollar bill and ask who wants the money. As I stand silently, people raise their hands and call out that they want the money. This goes on for a few minutes as the various audience members try to get my attention. Eventually, someone stands and walks to the front of the room and takes the money from my hand. When I ask the other audience members what stopped them from taking the action necessary to become a hundred dollars richer, the response is usually something like, "I wanted to, but I thought you would say no," or "I was afraid to look stupid," or "It just didn't cross my mind to take the one action needed."

When a problem comes your way that you need to fix, make sure it *does* cross your mind to take action. Stay solution oriented, and narrow your focus to the present and what you can do now (or in the immediate future) to make yourself a better, more complete athlete. Let yourself believe that every problem comes with a viable solution. And don't allow yourself to believe that you won't be able to figure out what you can do to make yourself better.

Make Success Permanent and Failure Temporary

A pitcher told me once, "There are times when no matter what I do, no matter how much I prepare or how well I pitch, I will lose. What really stinks is that I can't control it." My response was, "That is certainly one way to look at it." I tend to disagree with any client of mine who claims to be unable to control his or her results. I believe that control is a positive force and is, more often than most people think, eminently attainable.

The pitcher who believes there are times when he doesn't have control is correct. One's reality becomes what one believes. Remember that you cannot outperform or underperform your self-image for long. So, if you believe you have the control to change and influence your results in every situation, you are also correct.

A three-step process carries you to experiencing success as a permanent state and failure as only temporary:

1. Decide what you want to accomplish and what it takes to get there (product and process goals).
2. Choose to act on the physical and mental plans needed to accomplish your goals (MP100 + 20).
3. One of two things happens—either you achieve your goals or you make adjustments to step one (relentless solution focus).

In tracing steps one, two, and three, you can guarantee yourself of being more successful. The course can be burdensome, especially when you're being tripped up at seemingly every turn; being great is hard work. It just so happens that ensuring success as a permanent state falls directly in line with subscribing to the 10-MT mental-training plan. If you will follow the three phases of 10-MT, you will be in *full* control of your success.

Bolster yourself. Surround yourself with people who want to scale the same heights. If your training companions are always complaining and wallowing in their problems, your solution focus is sure to waver. Have you ever had the experience of hearing a song and then that song plays in your head all day? People internalize the words they hear and the images they see. If you commune with people who are goal driven and who emphasize solutions, it will be easier to internalize the positive thinking to which you're exposed. If you want to have a great attitude, you have to train yourself to have a great attitude.

Most athletes know the importance of having a positive attitude; it's just that carrying out a positive mind-set at times strains the resources. Tracy Steel, a former coach of mine, had a military background, which he combined with an intense positive attitude to create highly motivational training environments. Coach Steel used to tell me, "To know and not do is to not yet know." Merely knowing that it's important to have a good attitude is not enough—you must actually live it.

The Secret Formula to Team Chemistry

We all know that team chemistry is a basic component of group success. What does team chemistry really mean, though? Every team has chemistry, but what determines helpful or successful team chemistry? Team chemistry is simply how members of a team interact with one another. Positive team chemistry is characterized by individuals working together in a way that produces a whole greater than the sum of its parts. In athletics, the team that works together will achieve more.

The 2006 St. Louis Cardinals and the 1999 St. Louis Rams are classic examples of teams that pulled together to optimize their ability to win even with the chips stacked against them. The fundamentals of team chemistry work with any type of team or group—whether it is a professional sports team, a Fortune 500 company, or your normal, everyday family.

If the individuals in a group utilize the solution-focused tools, they will be more successful as individuals. One of the best attributes of a solution-focused team is that members can rely on each other to promote solution-focused thinking. For years, people have tried to control and develop team chemistry. Team-building books, workshops, and strategies are common and helpful. However, all this modern-age information is complicated and requires time to learn and digest. Many teams don't have the luxury of acquiring and instituting the latest and greatest method of developing team chemistry. The good news is that developing positive team chemistry can be boiled down to one directive: challenge each member to develop a relentless solution focus.

I reiterate: when members of a group are solution focused, they will be more successful as individuals. They will have positive attitudes and will enjoy the everyday challenges that arise, because they will have the knowledge and self-belief that they can overcome any problem, big or small, that comes up.

Attitudes are contagious; people tend to take on the attitudes and actions of the individuals in their circle. A good attitude is just as contractible as a bad one. If you habitually conduct yourself with a solution focus, those around you will start to follow your model. Do you think a team full of solution-focused players would have favorable chances of winning? Bet on it. If winning appeals to you, then play your part by taking a relentless approach to becoming and staying solution focused.

If individuals on a team will work together, there will be more positive team chemistry. It is natural for individuals to work against themselves and each other. When we feed into problems, the problems expand. However, once people begin airing possible solutions, the outlook brightens immediately. Some people will resist being solution focused because it is foreign. Do not let that resistance hold sway. Until there is a solution on the board, continue to ask, "What is one thing we can do that would make this better?" Pose the question often enough that your team becomes adept at fielding it and tossing it around.

An illustration of the profound impact a solution-focused mentality can have on a team is the Marshall University football program. In 1970, the majority of the team and coaching staff were killed in a terrible plane crash. In the wake of the tragedy, the university and the town of Huntington, West Virginia, were devastated. Many of the mourners were in favor of suspending the football program indefinitely.

In an attempt to help the town and university work through the abiding despair, the university's president decided to continue with the football program's rich tradition. The new head coach, Jack Lengyel, faced severe obstacles to success. It was a mammoth task just to field a team, much less be competitive. Coach Lengyel was undaunted by the barriers in his team's path. He armed himself with a solution-focused attitude that eventually was replicated throughout the team and campuswide. The players, the coaches, the university administrators, and eventually the townspeople gradually converted to the coach's never-quit attitude. And the Marshall football team returned to its winning ways.

CHAPTER 11

Mental Toughness

Knowing What and How to Think

I consider an individual to be mentally tough when the mind is in control of thoughts that help the body accomplish what is wanted. Mental toughness comes in assorted packages. Tyler McIlwraith's relentless pursuit of what it takes to stay one step ahead of her competition is proof of her mental toughness. During practices and games, Tyler replays in her mind the thoughts and images that incite her to play aggressively and confidently. Sean Townsend's mental toughness is most obvious in pressure situations. Sean rises to the challenge of competition and is able to keep his mind totally on the present. He approaches each routine "one skill at a time."

Many athletes and coaches believe that mental toughness is something that can be accomplished without mental training. I have had countless coaches tell me they expect their players to be mentally tough, even though they have no real mental-conditioning program to speak of. Regardless of how you define mental toughness, do yourself the favor of figuring out what thoughts help you perform. Then, flush with that knowledge, start improving your ability to maintain those thoughts during training and competition. The 10-MT program will begin helping you once you become accountable for your thoughts and actions and their influence on your results. You *choose* your success by what you think and what you do.

When problems knock you for a loop, don't feel sorry for yourself or make excuses. Get your mind tuned to what you want to accomplish, get a firm handle on what it will take to achieve your goals, and then get busy. Begin the physical and mental work needed to get yourself past obstacles you encounter. Here I refer you to what Coach Bobby Bowden told Lou Holtz after Bobby's West Virginia team beat Lou's William and Mary squad by a score of 41–7. Coach Holtz complained, "Bobby, I thought we were friends. How could you let your team keep piling on points like that?" Bowden responded, "Lou, it's your job to keep the score down. . . . If you don't want to get beat badly, get better athletes, coach better, or change the schedule."

If you want to rise higher in sports and in life, it is your responsibility to do what it takes to make it happen. Do not waste your breath or brain cells on cursing the unfairness and difficulty of your plight. Appoint goals, equip yourself with a mental workout that emphasizes what it takes to achieve those goals, and then don't let anyone or anything stop you. As part and parcel, you will naturally become more solution focused in pressure situations and rough patches. You will become mentally strong enough to replace self-doubt and negativity with positive self-talk and visualization. The more you choose to think about what you want and what it takes to get there, the more success you will reap. Let's review how the three phases of 10-MT can help you choose the right mental attitude.

Phase 1: The Mental Workout

The mental workout is a five-step process that I want you to complete every day before training and competition.

Step 1: Centering Breath

The centering breath is a fifteen-second breath in which you breathe in for six seconds, hold for two, and then breathe out for seven. In doing so, you will biologically control your heart rate so as to better control your arousal state and ability to think under pressure.

Step 2: Performance Statement

After taking your centering breath, repeat to yourself the statement that most effectively focuses you on what it takes for you to be successful in competition. Repeating the performance statement in your mental workout will help remind you of the most helpful thought necessary for success.

Step 3: Personal Highlight Reel

After reciting your performance statement, spend about three minutes visualizing what it looks like to be successful. The personal highlight reel is your own "SportsCenter" highlight sequence, in which you get to watch yourself competing at your peak and living your dreams. The three, sixty-second parts of your personal highlight reel are replaying past success, imagining success in an upcoming elevated-pressure game or competition, and watching the next scheduled game or event in which you will compete. See yourself focusing on your performance statement as you go through your personal highlight reel. Emphasize visualizing from the third camera angle—as if your eyes are the camera lens; pay attention to how you want to feel physically and emotionally during warm-ups and competition; visualize at game speed; and spend a little time imagining the result you want.

Step 4: Identity Statement

Upon completing your personal highlight reel, repeat to yourself your identity statement to help mold your self-image. The identity statement is a proven tool for boosting self-confidence, which is the single most helpful mental variable in improving performance. If you think you can, you have a much better shot at doing. You can feed your self-confidence by consistently reminding yourself of your greatest strength and your capacity to accomplish great things. Whatever you tell yourself, you are correct. If you continually tell yourself that you can and will accomplish your dreams, you will starkly increase the likelihood of having it happen. Conversely, the more you allow yourself to engage in self-doubt, the more difficult and unlikely it will be to make your dreams a reality.

Step 5: Centering Breath

The mental workout ends the way it begins, with a fifteen-second deep breath. This breath resets your heart rate to a level of controlled arousal and increased mental focus. Completing the personal highlight reel can cause the heart rate and arousal state to rise. By taking the final centering breath and staying relaxed until the action moments of training and competition, you make it easier to perform well.

Phase 2: Goal Setting for Greatness

The 10-MT goal-setting program helps individuals develop a work ethic that contributes to being *fully* prepared for competition. It has almost become a cliché for athletes to say, "I am trying." I believe that if you feel the need to announce that you are trying, you probably need to find a way to try harder. "I am trying" is what folks say when they are not accomplishing what they set out to do. Telling yourself and others that you are trying distracts you from thinking about what you need to do differently. Next time, instead of falling back on "I am trying," ask yourself, "What is one thing I can do that could make this better?"

The hallmark of 10-MT goals is doing everything you can do to increase the likelihood of your success. Athletes must learn to toe the fine line of doing what is needed without overdoing it. Most of us aren't at risk of overtraining, but since it can be just as unproductive as undertraining, you should be aware of the symptoms:

Symptoms of Physical Overtraining

- Frequent injury
- Unhealthy weight loss
- Reduced strength
- Frequent or lingering sickness

Symptoms of Mental Overtraining

- Increased memory problems
- Unmanageable stress or anxiety
- Headaches
- Sleep disturbances

Please speak with your coach if you suspect you are overtraining. Let your coach help you decide if your training is unhealthy and what you can do about it.

Try to set goals to promote the MP100 + 20 rule of following with diligence and intensity 100 percent of the physical-training plan your coach sets for you and 100 percent of the mental-training plan outlined in this book. Once you are consistently doing everything your coaches advise, search for ways to add your own ideas to your training. Push yourself 20 percent further to ensure that you are more prepared for the competition than they are for you. You will feel truly ready for greatness, and your confidence will soar.

When setting goals, emphasize process over product. Process goals are essential for identifying what it takes on a daily basis to achieve greatness. Keep focusing on what it will take on your part to be successful, rather than just envisioning the successful outcome. It is A-OK to think about product goals outside of training and competition, but once the action begins, lock into a pinpoint focus on your process goals.

When you know what you want to accomplish, write it down, and spread the word. Talking about your goals will spring them from your subconscious into your consciousness. It will also add to your accountability. It is harder to call it quits if you have publicly declared that nothing will stop you.

Become a "no-excuses" athlete. If you come up short on your goals, avoid giving the reasons why. Simply tell yourself and anyone else who is interested that you missed the mark and you will work on improving and doing better next time. Accountability is a tremendously powerful tool for growth—and excuses are the number one obstacle to accountability.

Above all, remember that goals work only if they are kept alive. I concede that it's demanding to commit to setting goals on a daily and weekly basis, but it's necessary. It doesn't need to be a complex task, though; in fact, the more complicated, the less effective. Use Success Logs to keep your daily training focused and precise. As best as you can, try to identify just one thing you want to improve prior to each training day. Let your Success Log dictate what facet of your daily training you emphasize in your mental workout. As you become accustomed to using goals, the quality of the goals will improve.

Phase 3: Adopt a Relentless Solution Focus

Anytime you are in the presence of adversity, ask yourself, "What is one thing I can do that could make this better?" Force yourself to give a substantive answer. ("I don't know" is not an answer that will help.) You do not need perfection; all you need is improvement. Keep asking yourself the question until your problem is no longer an issue. Follow two simple rules to ensure success—Rule number one: Never, ever give up. Rule number two: Follow rule number one.

You and only you decide how successful you will be in sport and in life. If you will commit yourself to staying focused on what you want and being relentless about going and getting it, you will be in control. It starts with your belief in yourself, the belief that you can accomplish anything. Unfortunately, it is difficult to be a believer if you haven't had any appreciable success yet. Don't worry; ultimately, you cannot fail if you will trust in the following series:

1. Decide what you want to accomplish and what it takes to get there (product and process goals).
2. Choose to act on the physical and mental plans needed to accomplish your goals (MP100 + 20).
3. One of two things happens—either you achieve your product goals or you make adjustment to your process goals (relentless solution focus).

Developing and then never abandoning a solution-focused attitude will guarantee that you will begin accomplishing great thing. The more success you experience, the easier it will be to stretch smaller steps into giant steps. Being a giant in any field is not supposed to be easy, but the status is available if you want it. You can choose to be permanently successful by maintaining the *relentless* solution focus.

How Do I Know If It's Working?

When I started working with the Cardinals, the front office wanted to know how to gauge if the sport psychology program was helpful. Obviously, in professional sports, results and winning are the most decisive measurements of success. The 10-MT mental-training program will help athletes improve results, but I also want you to realize that there will be additional benefits. I understand that in both

The Five-Point Star of Mental Toughness

1. **Create your mental workout.** I find that it is best to develop your mental workout approximately two weeks prior to the beginning of preseason practices.
2. **Identify vision, product, and process goals.** It's usually preferable to complete the Goal Setting for Greatness Work Sheet during the week before preseason practices begin.
3. **Complete Success Logs every practice day.** As a conclusion to practice and competitions, spend two to three minutes recapping what went well and what you would like to improve for the next day.
4. **Do your mental workout before every practice and game.** If you can conjure three to five minutes daily before practice or competition to complete your mental workout, your mind will be much more focused on what it takes for you to be successful. Be sure to look over your previous day's Success Log to emphasize critical areas of improvement.
5. **Develop a relentless solution focus.** Commit to replacing all thoughts of weakness or self-doubt with thoughts and images of what it takes to be successful and what it feels like to be successful.

sport and life, what most people want is to win. I am all for that, and I want you to expect 10-MT to help you accomplish more in terms of results. Additionally, I want you to use a few other evaluation categories in your quest for success. Please let these criteria help you determine how well you are doing:

1. Improved work ethic
2. Ability to focus on performance cues (performance and identity statements) in training
3. Ability to focus on performance cues (performance and identity statements) in competition

4. Increased happiness and satisfaction (the solution-focused attitude will really help with this)
5. Improved performance (measure results with improvement rather than perfection)

My experience over the last ten years tells me hands-down that if you will follow the steps detailed in this book, you will absolutely show improvement in the measurements of success listed here. You will become mentally tougher, happier, and more successful. I have never known an athlete, executive, or individual who followed the 10-MT program and did not experience significant improvement.

Each day, in the time it takes to hard-boil an egg, you can develop the mental edge needed to reach and exceed your potential. Are you willing to commit the time needed to put yourself in the best position to be successful? Ten minutes per day can change your life and send you off to capture your dreams. It takes a special person to make this commitment, a person who has the courage to claim the spotlight and is willing to do what is necessary to succeed.

Whether you are a young athlete just getting started, a weekend warrior trying to recapture your glory years, or a seasoned veteran, 10-Minute Toughness will help. Now that you have an understanding of what a competent mental-training plan entails, I want you to feel comfortable making adjustments and customizing the details to better suit your needs. Even if you are a businessperson or student, these tools and principles still apply and can toughen you up and help you meet your challenges head on. If there is anything I can ever do to assist you in your endeavors, please let me know—I would love to help.

Appendix A

Mental Training Through the Year

Now that you have all the details of the 10-MT mental exercise program down pat, you need to smoothly incorporate 10-MT into your regular training schedule. To guide you, I've placed the mental preparation into a twelve-month training cycle based on the widely accepted method of training periodization.

Periodization

Periodization divides the athlete's year into four phases of competition, as they relate to the competitive schedule:

- **Postseason.** This phase begins immediately after the last competitive event of the season and lasts for approximately two months. During this interval, it is restorative for athletes to get away from the sport both physically and mentally. From a mental standpoint, I encourage athletes to stop doing mental workouts altogether in this phase. This is a good time to give the body and mind a rest.

  If you happen to be making an immediate transition into another sport, it would be appropriate to complete a new Goal Setting for Greatness Work Sheet. Likewise, you should continue using daily Success Logs and create a new mental workout for the upcoming sport participation. This is also a prime opportunity to commit to maintaining the relentless solution focus.

- **Generalized preparatory.** In this next phase, athletes apply themselves to general strength, flexibility, speed, agility, and cardiovascular training. For the duration, typically three to four months, athletes need to emphasize a strong conditioning base to ensure that as they move into the next training cycle, they will avoid injury and increase skill-development potential. This is a good time to complete the Goal Setting for Greatness Work Sheet and develop a season-specific mental workout. In this phase, athletes may want to start doing their mental workouts two or three times per week to supplement the strength and conditioning programs they are undertaking. The details of the mental workout should reflect the current training that the athlete is following. Also, there's no time like the present to commit to maintaining the relentless solution focus.
- **Specialized preparation.** In this phase, which lasts anywhere from a month to two months, athletes emphasize skill-specific strength and conditioning. This is a golden opportunity to recommit to mental preparation. If athletes haven't already completed the Goal Setting for Greatness Work Sheet and Mental Workout Work Sheet for reference in the season to come, better get to it. In this phase, it would be ideal for athletes to go through their mental workouts three to five times per week and to begin filling out Success Logs after training sessions and reviewing them prior to mental workouts. If you haven't done so already, or noticed the pattern, it is incumbent on you to commit now to maintaining the relentless solution focus.
- **Competitive in-season.** We've come to the main competitive season within the twelve-month cycle. Athletes

will benefit from doing their mental workouts daily before training and competition (five to seven times per week) and from filling out Success Logs after every practice or competition and reviewing them prior to the next day's mental workout. As ever, if your commitment is at all shaky, renew your vow to maintain the relentless solution focus.

Examples

To illustrate, here are timelines for two athletes with whom I work that embody the general event milestones of their respective sports:

Professional Baseball Player

- **Generalized preparatory:** December 1–February 15

  December 1: Core physical training resumes. Athlete will engage in mental workout two or three times per week to prepare for strength and conditioning programs.

  January 15: Athlete completes season-specific Mental Workout Work Sheet.

  January 20: Athlete completes Goal Setting for Greatness Work Sheet.
- **Specialized preparation:** February 15–April 1

  February 15: Athlete reports to spring training, completing Success Logs each day after practices and preseason games. Athlete goes through mental workouts two or three times per week, before practice (emphasizing desired improvements from Success Logs).
- **Competitive in-season:** April 1–November 1

  April 1: Opening day. Athlete goes through mental workouts daily before practices and games (emphasizing desired improvements from daily Success Log entries).

- **Postseason:** November 1–December 1

  October/November 1: Season ends (varies year to year). No mental workouts during this phase, except for the commitment to the relentless solution focus addressing the shortcomings of the previous season in the season to come.

Professional Football Player

- **Generalized preparatory:** April 1–July 25

  April 1: Core physical training resumes. Athlete will engage in mental workout two or three times per week to prepare for strength and conditioning programs.

  July 15: Athlete completes season-specific Mental Workout Work Sheet.

  July 20: Athlete completes Goal Setting for Greatness Work Sheet.

- **Specialized preparation:** July 25–September 1

  July 25: Training camp begins. Athlete completes Success Logs each day after practices and scrimmages. Athlete does mental workouts two or three times per week, before practices (emphasizing desired improvements from Success Logs).

- **Competitive in-season:** September 1–February 1

  September 1: Season begins. Athlete goes through mental workouts daily before practices and games (emphasizing desired improvements from daily Success Log entries).

- **Postseason:** February 1–April 1

  January/February 1: Season ends (varies year to year). No mental workouts during this phase, except for the commitment to a relentless solution focus addressing the shortcomings of the previous season in the season to come.

Appendix B

Work Sheets

Goal Setting for Greatness Work Sheet

1. **What are the three greatest priorities in your life? (Please list them in order of importance.)**

   ____

   ____

   ____

   Create an image in your mind of what you would like your life to be like ten years in the future, including as much detail as possible related to your three greatest priorities.

   ____

   ____

   ____

   ____

   ____

   ____

   ____

   ____

   ____

2. **What is your ultimate goal in sport? (Be sure your ultimate goal has vision integrity.)**

   ____

   ____

   ____

3. **List one product goal for the upcoming season and three process goals needed to accomplish it:**

Product goal: ____

Process goal: ____

Process goal: ____

Process goal: ____

4. **List a second product goal for the upcoming season and three process goals needed to accomplish it:**

Product goal: ____

Process goal: ____

Process goal: ______________________________

____

____

Process goal: ______________________________

____

____

5. **Describe a material or experiential incentive you will use to reward yourself once you accomplish your season product goal.**

____

____

____

____

____

6. **List the sacrifices it will take on your part for you to achieve your ultimate sport goal.**

____

____

7. **List your character traits that show proof that you have what it takes to achieve your ultimate sport goal.**

____

____

8. **Name a coach or mentor who will review your goals progress by the fifth of every month.**

____

10-MINUTE TOUGHNESS

The Mental Workout Work Sheet

The five parts of my 10-MT mental workout are:

1. ______________________________
2. ______________________________
3. ______________________________
4. ______________________________
5. ______________________________

The time it takes me to complete my centering breath is: __________

The one most important thought that helps me compete at my best is (this is my performance statement):

____

My ideal arousal state is: __________

The three parts of my personal highlight reel (including specific highlights) are:

Part 1: Past Success ______________________________

- ______________________________
- ______________________________
- ______________________________
- ______________________________
- Personal greatest moment in sport (freeze-frame photo): __________

____

Part 2: Next Elevated-Pressure Competition/Game (emphasize feeling your performance statement and ideal arousal state) ______

- ______
- ______
- ______
- ______
- ______

Part 3: Next Competition/Game (emphasize feeling your performance statement and ideal arousal state) ______

- ______
- ______
- ______
- ______
- ______

The self-image statement that reminds me that I have what it takes to be a great athlete is (this is my identity statement):

______

The best times for me to complete my mental workout (centering breath—performance statement—personal highlight reel—identity statement—centering breath) are:

______

10-MINUTE TOUGHNESS

Success Log

"I've always believed that if you put in the work, the results will come. I don't do things half-heartedly. Because I know if I do, then I can expect half-hearted results."

—Michael Jordan

1. What three things did I do well today?

▶ ____

____

▶ ____

____

▶ ____

____

2. Based on today's performance, what do I want to improve?

____

____

3. What is one thing I can do differently that could lead to the desired improvement?

____

____

____

____

Notes

Chapter 1

1. Bob Rotella with Bob Cullen, *The Golfer's Mind: Play to Play Great*. New York: Free Press, 2004.

Chapter 2

1. Linda Bunker, Jean M. Williams, and Nate Zinsser, "Cognitive Techniques for Improving Performance and Building Confidence," in *Applied Sport Psychology: Personal Growth to Peak Performance* (2nd ed.), edited by Jean M. Williams. Mountain View, CA: Mayfield Publishing, 1993.
2. Steven Ungerleider, *Mental Training for Peak Performance*. Emmaus, PA: Rodale Press, 1996, p. 238.
3. Jim Taylor and Greg Wilson, *Applying Sport Psychology: Four Perspectives*. Champaign, IL: Human Kinetics, 2005.

Chapter 3

1. Alan Cohen, *Relax into Wealth: How to Get More by Doing Less*. New York: Tarcher, 2006.
2. Jack Canfield, *The Success Principle: How to Get from Where You Are to Where You Want to Be*. New York: Collins, 2005.
3. Ben Hogan, *Five Lessons: The Modern Fundamentals of Golf*. New York: Simon & Schuster, 1957.

Chapter 4

1. Thomas Boswell, "It Doesn't Take a Genius to Beat Tiger," *Washington Post*, washingtonpost.com/wp-dyn/content/article/2007/04/08/AR2007040801230.html. Accessed April 2007.

2. Claire Smith, "Born Again . . . and Born to Win with God on His Side," *The Scotsman*, http://news.scotsman.com/international.cfm?id=548872007. Accessed May 2007.
3. ASAP Sports interview with Zach Johnson, asapsports.com/show_interview.php?id=42431. Accessed April 2007.
4. Maxwell Maltz, *The New Psycho-Cybernetics*. New York: Prentice Hall, 2001.

Chapter 5

1. Kay Porter, *The Mental Athlete*. Champaign, IL: Human Kinetics, 2003.

Chapter 6

1. Stephen Covey, *The 8th Habit: From Effectiveness to Greatness*. New York: Free Press, 2004.

Chapter 7

1. Gary Mack, *Mind Gym: An Athlete's Guide to Inner Excellence*. New York: McGraw-Hill, 2001.

Glossary

Always have a solution on the board: A results-driven model that identifies and helps overcome all biological and environmental obstacles to achieving greatness.

Arousal state: The level of energy or excitement an athlete experiences during performance.

Can't say "I don't know" game: A solution-based tool that forces participants to get in a problem-solving mode by prohibiting them from giving "I don't know" as an answer.

"Don't" thinking: An ineffective series of thoughts in which the athlete focuses on what he or she does not want to do rather than what should be done.

Experiential reward: A reward that emphasize a positive experience. Examples include taking a cruise and spending a day at the spa.

Material reward: A tangible item that is a desirable possession. Examples include a new watch, a clothing item, cash, and even a new car.

MP100 + 20: A training approach that requires completing 100 percent of both mental-training and physical-training routines plus 20 percent above and beyond the status quo.

Muscle memory: A successful sequence of muscle contractions that can be consistently repeated during athletic performance.

Personal incentive style: Incentives that are congruent with an individual's personal reward preferences.

Personal Rewards Program Questionnaire: Questionnaire that identifies the athlete's motivational preferences.

+1 concept: The idea that success can be achieved by meeting a string of basic, incremental goals in the present that will ultimately lead to excellence in the future.

Process goal: The daily action needed to accomplish both product- and vision-level goals.

Product goal: A result-oriented goal that is clearly measurable and is usually most effective if it emphasizes accomplishments in the next twelve months.

Self-image: The level of success a person believes he or she is capable of achieving.

Success Log: Questions that encourage the identification of personal strengths and specific desires for improvement.

Ultimate goal: The culmination of what you want to accomplish and how you want to accomplish it.

Vision clarity: Ultimate goal accomplishment associated with sport.

Vision integrity: An attribute of goals aligning a person's hopes and dreams for the future with positive daily decisions.

What is one thing I can do that could make this better?: A concrete method of overcoming all obstacles and making success a permanent state.

Index